At Home in Her Tomb

Lady Dai and the Ancient Chinese Treasures of Mawangdui

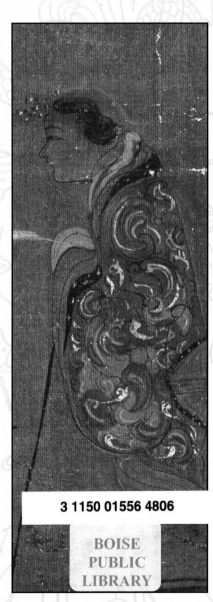

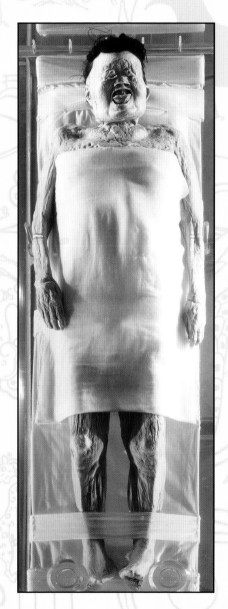

Christine Liu-Perkins 家 *with illustrations by* Sarah S. Brannen

Charlesbridge

To my father and mother, and our ancestors

Text copyright © 2014 by Christine Liu-Perkins
Illustrations copyright © 2014 by Sarah S. Brannen
Photographs copyright © Hunan Provincial Museum. Used with permission.
Translations of poems on pages 35 and 43 copyright © 1985 by David Hawkes. Used with permission.
All rights reserved, including the right of reproduction in whole or in part in any form.
Charlesbridge and colophon are registered trademarks of Charlesbridge Publishing, Inc.

Published by Charlesbridge
85 Main Street
Watertown, MA 02472
(617) 926-0329
www.charlesbridge.com

Library of Congress Cataloging-in-Publication Data
Liu-Perkins, Christine.
  At home in her tomb : Lady Dai and the ancient Chinese treasures of Mawangdui / Christine Liu-Perkins ; illustrated by Sarah S. Brannen.
    p. cm.
  Includes bibliographical references and index.
  ISBN 978-1-58089-370-1 (reinforced for library use)
  ISBN 978-1-60734-725-5 (ebook)
  ISBN 978-1-60734-615-9 (ebook pdf)
1. Mawangdui Site (China)—Juvenile literature. 2. Excavations (Archaeology)—China—Changsha (Hunan Sheng)—Juvenile literature. 3. Tombs—China—Changsha (Hunan Sheng)—Juvenile literature. 4. Human remains (Archaeology)—China—Changsha (Hunan Sheng)—Juvenile literature. 5. Treasure troves—China—Changsha (Hunan Sheng)—Juvenile literature. 6. Material culture—China—Changsha (Hunan Sheng)—Juvenile literature. 7. Changsha (Hunan Sheng, China)—Antiquities—Juvenile literature. 8. China—History—Han dynasty, 202 B.C.–220 A.D.—Juvenile literature.
I. Brannen, Sarah S., ill. II. Title.
DS797.52.M393L58 2013
931'.215—dc23   2012024630

Printed in Singapore
(hc) 10 9 8 7 6 5 4 3 2

Illustrations done in watercolor on Saunders cold-press paper
Display type and text type set in Adobe Garamond Pro and ITC Goudy Sans
Color separations by KHL Chroma Graphics, Singapore
Printed by Imago in Singapore
Production supervision by Brian G. Walker
Designed by Martha MacLeod Sikkema

Front Cover Photos
Top: The body of Lady Dai. *Bottom:* A modern painting of Lady Dai's funeral. *Background:* Silk brocade found in Lady Dai's tomb.
Hunan Provincial Museum

Title Page Photos
Left: A statue of Lady Dai showing how she might have looked as a young woman. *Center:* A portrait of Lady Dai as an old woman from the *feiyi* silk painting found on top of her innermost coffin. *Right:* The body of Lady Dai. *Background:* Line drawings of the images from Lady Dai's *feiyi*.
Hunan Provincial Museum

Table of Contents

Introduction

Face-to-Face with Lady Dai

In the peaceful stillness of the museum, I looked down through a window into a room below my feet. There lay a woman, face-up, draped in white silk. She appeared to be sleeping. But this woman had been "sleeping" for more than two thousand years. I had seen mummies before, but those were dry, skin-covered skeletons—not like this soft-fleshed body. I could not stop staring at her, Lady Dai from the Mawangdui tombs.

I wished I could wake her. I wanted to ask, "What was your life like? What did you enjoy doing? What did you like to eat?"

More than two millennia ago, Lady Dai lived, died, and was buried in a lavish tomb, next to the tombs of her husband and son. Now her body lies in the Hunan Provincial Museum in the city of Changsha in south-central China.

Seeing Lady Dai made me feel as though I were meeting an actual person from the distant past. Suddenly the museum's artifacts from the tombs became more than just ancient objects to me. I imagined Lady Dai looking into her bronze mirror and applying powder and rouge from the cosmetic boxes. I pictured her slipping her arms into the red robe and tying the laces of the silk socks behind her ankles.

Several displays included actual food from Lady Dai's tomb—still identifiable after thousands of years. I visualized her sitting on the floor, eating dinner off the lacquer dishes. I wondered what the fruits and grains would have tasted like, and how fragrant grasses burning under the cone-shaped basket would have smelled.

Seeing the silk books, the musical instruments, and the board game from the son's tomb made me ponder. Which of the books was his favorite? Did he often take breaks to play melodies on his zither? Did he and his mother ever play games of *liubo* together, taking turns rolling the eighteen-sided die?

The next day I eagerly traveled to the eastern side of Changsha to see the excavation site. Two of the tombs have been covered over and made into small parks. But the third remains open. I walked along a narrow path, entered a low brick building, and examined a few small displays. Then I stepped into a dark room—and stared down, down, down into the enormous pit of the tomb.

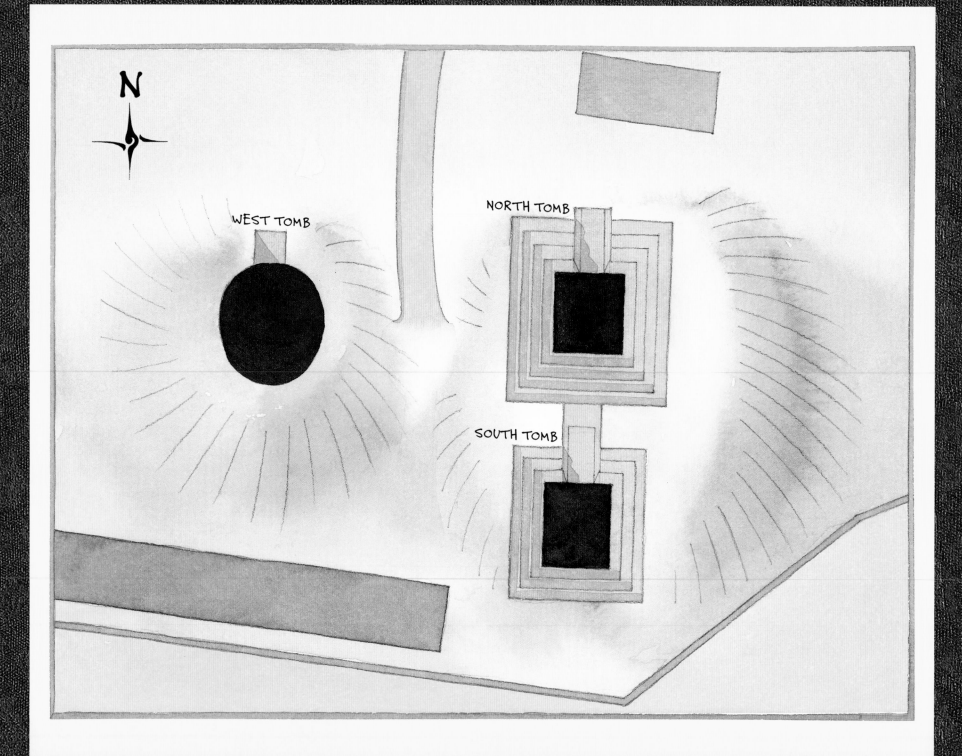

1

Excavation of a Time Capsule

For more than two thousand years, people had gazed across the plains at the pair of hills rising like a giant saddle from the earth. No ordinary hills, these were burial mounds covering supposedly royal tombs. But who was buried beneath them? Was it a prince of the Han dynasty and his mother, or perhaps the prince's mother and another royal lady? Or were the hills called Mawangdui, meaning "Mounds of King Ma," for a medieval king buried beneath them?

The truth would come as a surprise, with even greater surprises awaiting those who opened the tombs.

For more than two thousand years, a saddle-shaped pair of hills hinted at tombs hidden underneath. But no one remembered who was buried in the tombs.

<small>HUNAN PROVINCIAL MUSEUM</small>

Discoveries and Mysteries

On a cold December day in 1971, workers were digging near the burial mounds to build an air-raid shelter for an army hospital. Unexpectedly, they struck white clay. Methane, or marsh gas, escaped through holes drilled into the clay, burning with blue flames when lit. Methane forms when organic material decomposes in the absence of air. Experts called in from the Hunan Provincial Museum realized that an ancient tomb had been discovered—possibly dating from as far back as the Han dynasty (206 BCE–220 CE).

On January 16, 1972, official excavation of the tomb began. Bulldozers removed part of the eastern hill, exposing the top of the tomb pit. The pit had been filled with packed-down dirt, which had to be removed by hand.

Digging for buried treasure often conjures up images of excitement—and dust—but as the wet spring weather arrived, rain, mud, weariness, and discouragement bogged down the excavation. The work became harder and harder as the pit grew deeper. The workers dug with hoes, spades, and shovels and carried the dirt out in bamboo baskets. They climbed in and out of the pit on wooden scaffolding made unstable and slippery by the rain and mud. Years later, Hou Liang, the director of the excavation team, recalled being down inside the tomb pit: "I joked, 'If we don't do well, we will all probably be buried in here.' But inside my heart, I was scared this might actually happen."

With only a few dozen workers, progress was slow. Mr. Hou appealed to local schools for help; in return for their labor, students would learn about archaeology. Each day a different high school sent students to the excavation site. Mr. Hou later remembered: "These young students' help was like a timely rain to give morale and support. When the students arrived every day, we arranged them in lines to transport the dirt. The speed of the excavation was greatly improved. The most difficult time was in the pouring rain. The students did not have raincoats; everyone was soaked like wet chickens. It was most noticeable when the bamboo baskets were leaking; mud covered their clothes, and you could not get rid of it. Some of the students were so eager to work that they used their hands to dig; their hands were bleeding from splinters from the bamboo baskets."

After clearing out the mud from the pit, the workers found a thick layer of white clay. This very sticky clay was often used in southern China to seal tombs to keep water out. It was difficult to shovel and remove. Underneath the clay was a layer of black charcoal, often used to waterproof tombs

Students from local high schools were recruited to assist in excavating the tomb pit. The rainy spring weather made the work muddy and difficult, but the students' help sped up the pace of removing tons of earth, clay, and charcoal. HUNAN PROVINCIAL MUSEUM

The tomb had a mound 13 feet (4 meters) high above ground level. The pit beneath the mound was 52 feet (16 meters) deep, starting with four steps at the top and narrowing down like a funnel to the bottom. The mound, the steps, and the large size of the tomb were signs that a person of high rank was buried there. A ramp on the north side of the tomb was used to move materials into the pit. At the bottom of the pit, a thick layer of white clay and a thinner layer of charcoal encased a wooden burial chamber. The burial chamber is shown here as it appeared after the bamboo mats and wooden lids on top of it were removed, revealing five inner compartments.

around Changsha during the Han dynasty. The charcoal weighed approximately eleven thousand pounds (five thousand kilograms) and filled four large trucks.

Next came a layer of bamboo mats. Written on one corner of each of the twenty-six mats was the Chinese word *jia,* meaning "home" or "family." Whose home was this? What could be inside it?

The workers lifted the bamboo mats and were astonished to see a massive, perfectly preserved wooden burial chamber about 22 feet (6.7 meters) long and 16 feet (4.9 meters) wide. The burial chamber was constructed of seventy enormous planks of cypress wood, some weighing more than a ton.

The workers removed the top of the burial chamber. Inside lay a treasure chest divided into five sections: a giant black coffin filled the center space, with compartments on all four sides. Starting with the side compartments, they unpacked treasure after treasure in exquisite condition. One expert lifted the lid off a beautiful black-and-red tureen. "Look at that!" he exclaimed. Slices of ancient lotus root floated in liquid, looking fresh enough to eat. Other people crowded in to see for themselves, marveling at the sight. Quickly the man snapped a photograph of it. But then the lotus pieces disappeared, dissolving into the water.

Next came the challenge of removing the huge black coffin. Using a crane, the workers lifted the coffin out of the burial chamber. They then transferred the coffin to the Hunan Provincial Museum on April 26, 1972.

At the museum a team of experts eagerly lifted the lid of the black coffin. Inside they found a second coffin, painted all over with swirling clouds and

The Chinese character for *jia* (pronounced *jyah*), meaning "home" or "family," was written on the bamboo mats that covered the burial chamber. This artist's representation of the character is modeled on the same word as it appeared, painted in red, on a lacquer pitcher in the burial chamber.

mythical creatures on a black background. Inside that coffin was a third coffin, with colorful images of paradise on a red background. Nested inside was yet another coffin. Unlike any coffin they had seen before, this one was decorated with embroidered silk and feathers.

Within the fourth coffin, half-immersed in yellow-brown fluid, lay a bundle of silk tied with nine silk ribbons. Here was the occupant of the tomb!

One expert was delighted to see ancient silk in such beautiful, brightly colored condition. He reached out to touch the silk, but—what was wrong? The silk was "as soft as tofu. It looked in sound shape but actually had rotted away." The team was eager to see the body within the bundle, but the silk could not be easily removed. They tried cutting a small hole through the silk, but then a ghastly stench rose up, forcing everyone to cover their noses.

The experts were baffled. If the body had decomposed more than two thousand years ago, how could it still smell so disgusting?

Over the next week they carefully cut away twenty layers of wrappings and clothing, enduring the horrible odor hour after hour. Finally came a startling sight—a woman's body with soft, moist skin. How could this be? Who was she?

Found among the woman's treasures was a signature seal bearing her name: Xin Zhui. Some of the objects from her tomb were inscribed with the words "[Owned by] the Family of the Marquis of Dai." A marquis was one of the highest aristocratic ranks. Dai was a county lying northeast of the city of Changsha. Could the mysterious woman have been the wife of a marquis?

The burial chamber had four side compartments filled with supplies and a central compartment with four coffins nested inside one another. A T-shaped silk painting covered the lid of the innermost coffin. Within that coffin, hidden within twenty layers of silk, lay the amazingly well-preserved body of a woman.

A Family Forgotten

In the process of excavating the lady's tomb, workers had discovered that methane was also escaping from beneath the southern end of her burial mound. Could this be from another tomb? Excited by the treasures found in the lady's tomb, archaeologists prepared to excavate both this south tomb and the tomb under the hill to the west.

On November 19, 1973, excavation began on the south tomb, which was rectangular like the first tomb but smaller. Soon, however, the archaeologists became concerned. The tomb had been damaged when the lady's tomb was built, and the protective white clay was missing from one corner.

As they feared, water had seeped into the tomb. The coffin had split, and only a skeleton remained of the body of a man around thirty years old. Fortunately, however, 1,684 wonderful treasures had been preserved, including silk books, maps, and paintings. One painting depicted a military leader with lines of soldiers and horse-drawn chariots. Weapons, military maps, and a black officer's cap were other clues that the man might have been a general. Since he died relatively young, perhaps he was killed in battle. Was he the son of the lady Xin Zhui in the first tomb? Unfortunately, no evidence of his name was to be found.

On December 18, 1973, excavation of the west tomb began. The tomb was large, like the lady's tomb, with an unusual oval shape. Sadly, it too had been damaged—by the building of the lady's tomb, by water leaking into the burial chamber, and by tunnels dug by grave robbers. The coffin had collapsed when its sides rotted. The body was gone. Lacquer, pottery, and bronze objects were found inside the tomb, but many items were broken.

Winter's snow and freezing temperatures made retrieval of the artifacts difficult. The workers feared the tomb might collapse. Then a man picked up two signature seals from the mud. The jade seal was engraved with the name "Li Cang." The bronze seal was engraved with the words "Seal of the Marquis of Dai."

History books speak of a Marquis of Dai named Li Cang who served as chancellor of the Changsha Kingdom at the beginning of the Han dynasty. If this was truly his tomb, then a third seal confirming his position as chancellor should have been buried with the other two seals. It must have fallen out of the collapsed coffin, but where was it? The team decided to lift up the bottom of the coffin and systematically search through the mud underneath it. They loaded the mud into baskets, carried them back to the museum, and carefully sifted through each load. At last it appeared: a bronze seal engraved with the title "Chancellor of Changsha."

The Marquis of Dai
Li Cang held the title of full marquis, the highest of twenty aristocratic ranks during the early Han dynasty. He was granted a marquisate by the emperor Han Huidi as a reward for his service. His title came with the large but relatively poor territory of Dai, a county within the kingdom of Changsha. Seven hundred families lived and worked the land in Dai, compared to more than ten thousand families in other fiefdoms.

As Li Cang's wife, Xin Zhui shared his rank. She is sometimes referred to as the Marquise or Marchioness of Dai, but more often as Lady Dai.

This bronze signature seal, which reads "Seal of the Marquis of Dai," helped confirm the identity of the man in the west tomb. He was Li Cang, the Marquis of Dai and the chancellor of Changsha at the beginning of the Han dynasty.
Hunan Provincial Museum

In this map of China during the early Han dynasty, the gold section shows the land ruled by the Han Empire. The orange section shows the Changsha Kingdom. The land owned by the Marquis of Dai lay in the northeastern part of the kingdom (between present-day Luoshan County and Guangshan County in Henan Province). The red dot marks the site of the three tombs.

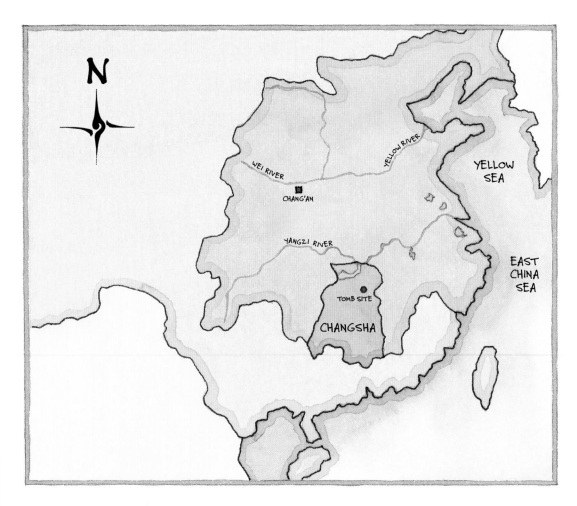

The Chancellor of Changsha
In Li Cang's time, the Han Empire was divided into ten kingdoms in the east and fourteen commanderies in the west. The highest official in each kingdom was a chancellor. As chancellor of Changsha, Li Cang was responsible for such duties as collecting taxes, keeping law and order, maintaining roads and canals, and defending the kingdom.

The freezing mud had yielded three crucial pieces of evidence in the mystery of Mawangdui. Piecing together the clues from the tombs with historical records, researchers were able to identify the family.

- **The Marquis:** As chancellor of the Changsha Kingdom, Li Cang held the highest position in the government under the king. He was made the Marquis of Dai by the emperor Han Huidi in 193 BCE. Records show that Li Cang died in 186 BCE.

- **The Lady:** Xin Zhui was the wife of Li Cang. Archaeologists know that she was the last of the three to be buried because the building of her tomb damaged the other two tombs. Scholars believe she died around 158 BCE at fifty-four years of age. She is often referred to as Lady Dai.
- **The Son:** The unnamed man in the south tomb, buried in 168 BCE, was the son of Li Cang and Xin Zhui. But which of their sons was he? Some experts believe he was Li Xi, the second Marquis of Dai. Others believe he was a different son. This puzzle of Mawangdui remains unsolved.

The Time Capsule Opened

The Li family lived at the beginning of the Han dynasty. Discovering their tombs was like opening an ancient time capsule assembled more than two thousand years ago. Hidden inside lay more than three thousand astonishingly well-preserved treasures that revealed rich, vivid details of life in China during the second century BCE. Some objects were the first or oldest of their type to be discovered.

Excitement about the Mawangdui artifacts spread around the world. Hundreds of thousands of people flocked to museum exhibits in China, the United States, the Netherlands, Japan, South Korea, Taiwan, Singapore, Italy, and France. Scholars of many countries continue to study the finds and have published nearly four thousand books and articles on their discoveries. The Mawangdui time capsule changed the world's knowledge of ancient China.

The most startling discovery of all was the body of Lady Dai. Historical records offer no information about her life. However, the body she left behind speaks volumes about her lifestyle and health—and even the cause of her death.

The Han Dynasty: A Model for Millennia

The empire of the Han dynasty is often compared to the Roman Empire. They overlapped in time, with the Han dynasty lasting from 206 BCE to 220 CE, and the Roman Empire from 200 BCE to 395 CE. They controlled territories of comparable size, with populations of approximately sixty million. Combined, they encompassed perhaps half of the world's inhabitants. Each empire ruled over multiple peoples, cultures, and lands within its borders.

The Han dynasty established a model for running a unified empire that lasted all the way into the twentieth century. (China's last emperor gave up the throne in 1912.) The success and stability of the Han Empire enabled China to expand into new territories, set up an educational system for training future government officials, and spawn new inventions (such as paper) that would have worldwide impact.

2

The Mysterious Cadaver

*L*ady Dai is in high spirits, enjoying a visit from her children and their families. The day is warm. A snack of juicy muskmelon is perfect for quenching her thirst.

Suddenly pain strikes in the soft space between her lower ribs. She has endured abdominal pains before, but this time is worse. After a few moments a different pain starts in her chest and moves upward. Her heart is beating too fast. She feels dizzy. The room seems to spin, and then everything goes dark.

The body of Xin Zhui was amazingly well preserved, even after being buried for almost 2,200 years. Her yellow-brown skin was still moist, and when pressed down, it bounced back. Her joints were still movable; when her arms were lifted, they bent at the elbows and rotated from the shoulder joints. When preservative was injected into her muscles, they swelled and then absorbed the preservative—like a recently dead body would. The patterns of her fingerprints and toe prints were clear.

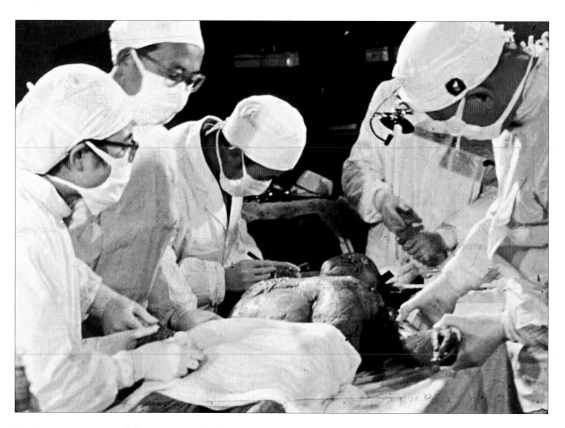

Dr. Peng Long-xiang (left, center) and other doctors from the Hunan Medical College (now called the Xiangya School of Medicine) conducted an autopsy on Lady Dai's body to find out the cause of her death and the state of her health when she died. Peng Long-xiang and the Hunan Provincial Museum

Examining the Body

Forty-four experts from almost every department of Hunan Medical College came together to study Xin Zhui's corpse. They joked that "only the pediatrician did not join the research team, because the ancient cadaver was an adult." Recognizing that this body could reveal much about the health of their ancient ancestors, they decided to conduct a pathological autopsy. How did the woman die? From what diseases did she suffer? The autopsy would hopefully answer these questions.

Experts from other cities joined them to plan the autopsy. They came up with other questions and a detailed procedure that would preserve the cadaver's outer appearance and internal organs for future exhibition. Peng Long-xiang, the chairman of the Department of Pathology at Hunan Medical College, volunteered to lead the autopsy team.

On December 14, 1972, Dr. Peng and his team performed the autopsy before an audience of government leaders, scientists, and other experts. Despite the observers, Dr. Peng wasn't nervous. "I wasn't thinking about all the important people in the room," he later recalled. "I just focused my mind on figuring out how this woman died." The doctors inspected and measured the outside of the body. They opened the head, chest, and abdomen. They examined each organ and took small samples for further study. They took X-rays and photographs.

The team discovered that Xin Zhui was about 5 feet, ½ inch (154 centimeters) tall and had weighed close to 150 pounds (68 kilograms) while she was alive (her cadaver weighed 75.5 pounds, or 34.3 kilograms). She was around fifty years old when she died. She wore a wig attached with hairpins

Is Lady Dai a Mummy?
Most often people think of a mummy as a dehydrated body. Many scientists, though, define a mummy as any dead body whose soft tissue has been preserved, either by natural or artificial means. (Soft tissue includes muscles, fat, ligaments, tendons, and blood vessels, but not bones.) According to this definition, Lady Dai's preserved body is indeed a mummy. But other scientists, such as Dr. Peng, head of the Mawangdui autopsy team, prefer the unique term "Mawangdui-type cadaver," as Lady Dai's body "differs from all other types of preserved cadavers reported in the past."

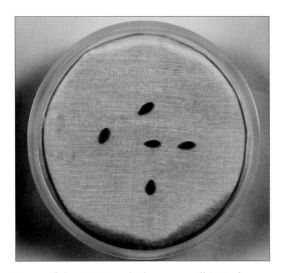

Some of the 138½ seeds that were still in Lady Dai's digestive tract—evidence that she ate melon shortly before she died. Hunan Provincial Museum

to her own hair. Her blood type was A. Only nineteen teeth (out of the normal thirty-two) remained in her mouth. She had suffered from many health problems, including general atherosclerosis (arteries narrowed by plaque buildup), serious heart disease, gallstones, tuberculosis, blood fluke parasites, pinworms, whipworms, lead and mercury accumulation, osteoporosis (loss of bone tissue), a degenerated spinal disc, and a broken right arm that had healed out of place.

How did she die? No signs were found of a fatal injury from an accident, murder, or suicide. However, a surprising discovery showed that she died about an hour after eating: 138½ muskmelon seeds remained undigested in her esophagus, stomach, and intestines. The doctors concluded that she had died of a sudden heart attack, perhaps triggered by a very painful episode of gallstones.

To Decompose . . . or Not

Usually after a person dies, the body decomposes. Its cells begin breaking down. Bacteria that live on the skin and inside the body—especially those that once helped digest food—now turn to destroying the corpse. Bacteria from the outside environment, fungi, flesh-eating insects, and scavenger animals can also speed up the destruction.

If decomposition is stopped, the body can be preserved. Sometimes this happens naturally. Air, sand, or salt can dehydrate a corpse, and cold temperatures can freeze or freeze-dry it. A number of bodies have been found in peat bogs in Europe, preserved through some combination of water, low oxygen, acidity, cold temperatures, and the chemicals in peat moss.

Humans have also developed artificial methods for preserving their dead, including embalmment, dehydration, and freezing. Elaborate processes have been used by people throughout the ages, including ancient Egyptians and Chinchorros (a people in South America), as well as Buddhist monks in China and Japan starting at the end of the third century. Nowadays, laboratories around the world preserve bodies by replacing fluids and fats with special plastics that make soft tissue rigid, a process called plastination. These modern mummies are displayed in museum exhibits and used for teaching in medical schools.

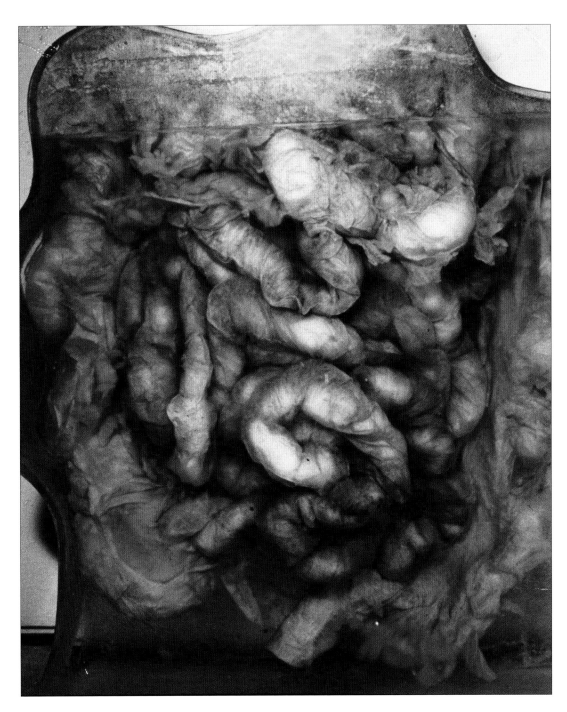

After the autopsy, some of Lady Dai's internal organs, including her intestines (seen in this photo), heart, stomach, lungs, and brain, were preserved in clear containers. HUNAN PROVINCIAL MUSEUM

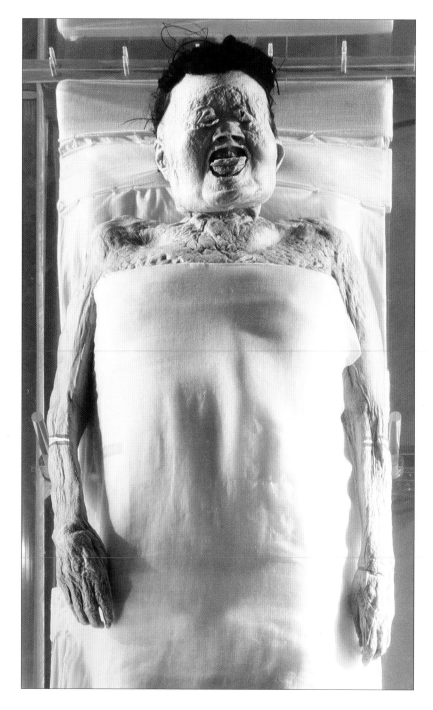

Preserving the Body

Lady Dai's body had actually started decomposing. Her tongue stuck out of her open mouth, and her eyeballs had begun falling out. But then somehow the bacteria that cause decay stopped growing. Why?

Chinese scientists believe that three major factors helped preserve her body. First, the careful preparation of the body for burial slowed the early stages of decomposition. As a member of the nobility, Lady Dai would have been washed with fragrant water and wine, which has antibacterial properties. Then many layers of clothes and shrouds were wrapped around her body.

Second, the body was placed in an airtight set of coffins. Without air, the existing bacteria slowed in growth and then died.

Third, the entire burial chamber was positioned deep underground, surrounded by charcoal and white clay. Water and air did not leak in. The body was protected from changes in the atmosphere and climate. The temperature stayed constantly cool.

Another possible factor is the fluid found in the

When it was discovered in 1972, the body of Lady Dai still had soft, moist skin and all its internal organs in place. HUNAN PROVINCIAL MUSEUM

innermost coffin. The source of this fluid is unknown, but many scientists believe it is water from the body, rather than liquid poured into the coffin. The acidic fluid may have helped preserve the body by preventing bacteria from growing.

No one knows for certain what combination of factors helped preserve Lady Dai's corpse, or why similar conditions failed to preserve other bodies. Yet even without a complete answer, we can still appreciate the amazing results.

Lady Dai has been called the "best preserved body in the world." At first glance she doesn't appear particularly beautiful or perfect in appearance. But through a microscope we can see that her corpse was preserved down to the level of cells, especially the cells of connective tissues like ligaments and tendons. She is so unusual that Chinese scientists developed the term "Mawangdui-type cadaver" to describe her body.

Xin Zhui's family meticulously applied methods that kept her body in remarkable condition. They were equally meticulous in preparing a tomb that would mirror her earthly life.

Other Mawangdui-Type Cadavers
Since the discovery of Lady Dai, a few other cadavers in similar condition have been found in China. Two come from the same time period as Xin Zhui; they belong to a male official named Sui Xiaoyuan and a noblewoman named Ling Huiping. However, no consistent pattern clearly explains why their bodies were preserved. All three had coffins containing liquid, but the liquid in Lady Dai's was acidic, inhibiting bacteria from growing, whereas the liquid in the others' was alkaline, which should have aided bacterial growth. The tombs were dug to different depths—from sixteen feet (five meters) to fifty-two feet (sixteen meters)—and contained different amounts of white clay and charcoal. Adding to the mystery, similar airtight and watertight seals failed to keep other bodies from decomposing into skeletons or dust.

3

A House Underground

Lady Dai's children rush to her side. "Mother!" they call. She does not respond. "She is not breathing. Her soul is leaving her body. We must call it back!" Desperately they spring into action.

They lay her on the ground and cover her with a sheet. A man designated as the summoner takes her robe to the roof of the house. Waving her garment, he calls out to her soul, "O Lady Dai, come back!" He calls again. He pauses before the third and final attempt. "O Lady Dai, come back!"

He casts her robe down to the designated receiver, who catches it in a basket and carries it into the mourning hall. "Does she live?"

The family members shake their heads. "No, she is gone from us." They place the garment over her body.

Wails of grief echo through the house.

What happens to us after we die? Does a part of us continue living? Is there an afterlife? Throughout history people all over the globe have come up with different answers to these questions.

Other questions involve the relationship between the living and the dead. How do we deal with the pain of missing loved ones? How do we show that they are not forgotten?

A Proper Farewell

During the Han dynasty people accepted many different, sometimes contradictory, ideas about what happened after a person died. Contrasting beliefs were often expressed side by side within a single tomb.

A fundamental idea was that human beings had a soul separate from the physical body. Some people believed in a single soul. After death this soul continued to exist in some form of consciousness and stayed in the grave with the body. The tomb served as the soul's underground home and was stocked with equipment and supplies for it.

Other people proposed that the soul had two parts: the *hun* and the *po*. The *hun* was the intelligent and spiritual part, and the *po* gave the body life. When a person died a normal death, these two parts of the soul separated. The *hun* traveled to a far-off destination—perhaps to heaven, to a paradise where immortals lived, to somewhere in the cosmos, or to the underworld. The *po* might travel, too, to a different part of the underworld or to a dark netherworld called the Yellow Springs—or it might stay with the body in the tomb.

If the *hun* and *po* traveled, the tomb served as a way station that provided supplies for the journey. If the *po* stayed, the tomb became its underground home. Although it could no longer make the body move or think, the *po* still needed to be kept happy and comfortable; otherwise it could return to the land of the living as an angry demon. There were various ways to appease the *po*. One was to bury in the grave such necessities as food, dishes, clothes, money, and models of servants and houses. Another was to protect the body from decay. Yet another was to regularly offer food and other items at the family shrine.

The largest of Lady Dai's decorated coffins displays swirling clouds and more than one hundred figures painted on a black background. Most of the figures are mythical animals engaged in human activities, such as playing musical instruments or capturing birds. Experts believe the clouds symbolize *qi* energy and the creatures represent spirits who would protect Lady Dai from evil. HUNAN PROVINCIAL MUSEUM

Family members, especially children, were expected to honor the dead. Filial piety, or love and respect for one's parents, was the central moral principle in Chinese culture long before the Han dynasty. The philosopher Confucius (551–479 BCE) is recorded as saying, "Filial piety is the root of virtue and the source of civilization." When a parent died, the children were expected to show deep grief and to provide a grave that demonstrated their devotion.

Preparing the Body

When death took Xin Zhui from them, her family would have followed extensive mourning and funeral rituals, as prescribed in the classic texts *Yili*

(*Etiquette and Rites*) and *Liji (Book of Rites)*. These rituals helped the family express their love and grief in culturally acceptable ways—and do all they could to satisfy the soul of the departed.

The first major ritual, "summoning the soul" or the "calling-back ceremony," was conducted right after someone appeared to have died. Death was thought to occur when the *hun* left the *po* and the body. But if the *hun* came back, then the person could go on living. A man—usually a family member or a servant—would have performed the ceremony by standing on the roof of the house and calling three times for Lady Dai's soul to return.

When this ritual failed to bring the soul back, the family had to accept that Lady Dai was truly dead. They washed her corpse and dressed it in layers of clothes and shrouds. They placed the shrouded body in a beautifully decorated coffin, which was then nested within three more coffins. One of the outer coffins had paintings of creatures believed to be spirits who would protect her from evil.

Preparing the Grave

Next the family made preparations for the tomb. The oldest son instructed a diviner, a type of fortune-teller, to determine that the gravesite was in a secure place safe from disaster, such as a landslide.

Once the site was approved, the builders dug an enormous pit fifty-two feet (sixteen meters) deep. They then laid three massive wooden beams across the bottom of the pit. On top of these beams, they constructed the burial chamber—an enormous box that represented a house. This was divided into five compartments—one in the center and four along the sides—simulating the rooms of the house.

Meanwhile the family prepared the furnishings and supplies that would be placed in the four side compartments. They continued to mourn the loss of their loved one.

When all was ready, the nested coffins were loaded onto a horse-drawn hearse for the funeral procession to the tomb site. Because Xin Zhui was the matriarch of a prominent family, the procession would have included a long line of people. Exorcists scaring off evil spirits, attendants displaying tablets and banners, servants carrying burial goods, musicians, family members, and more would have joined Lady Dai in her journey.

This modern painting captures what Lady Dai's funeral might have looked like. Mourners carrying banners walk down the ramp into the burial pit, where the body of Lady Dai would be placed in a massive wooden chamber. Hunan Provincial Museum

At the gravesite the coffins were lowered into the central compartment of the burial chamber. Then the other rooms were outfitted with everything Lady Dai's soul would need to be comfortable.

The north compartment, at Lady Dai's head, represented her personal living area. Silk curtains hung from the walls, and bamboo mats covered the floor. Lacquer dishes held food and drink. Wooden figurines of servants, musicians, dancers, and singers waited to serve and entertain Lady Dai's soul. A space was made for her soul to sit, surrounded by personal objects she had used in her daily life, including her cane. Two round lacquer boxes held the seal revealing her name, as well as cosmetics, a wig, combs, and a bronze mirror.

The other three side compartments functioned as storerooms. They were packed with food, dishes, clothing, herbal medicines, musical instruments, and even imitation coins made of clay. One hundred additional figurines of servants were placed in these compartments to care for Lady Dai's soul.

A double lid covered the entire chamber like the roof of a house. Workers filled the tomb pit with charcoal,

The north compartment (top) of the burial chamber contained a banquet scene. The other three side compartments functioned as storerooms filled with servant figurines, food, clothing, dishes, and other supplies. HUNAN PROVINCIAL MUSEUM

sticky white clay, and layers of earth, pounding down each layer until it was hard. Finally more earth was piled over the tomb pit, forming a hill.

A Lasting Farewell

The entire sequence of preparations would have taken days or even weeks to complete. At various times throughout the process, the family would have also performed ritualized wailing and offered sacrifices of food to Lady Dai's soul. While they mourned they would have worn rough hemp clothing and eaten plain foods, reflecting their inner grief and pain. For Lady Dai's children, formal mourning for their mother was to last three years.

Lady Dai's children demonstrated their love and respect by preparing a durable new home for her, lavishly stocked with the luxuries she had enjoyed in her earthly life. When archaeologists finally opened her burial chamber, the perfect time capsule astounded them.

4

All the Comforts of Home

Kneeling on a rush mat, Lady Dai breathes in the aromas of the food on the lacquer dishes. She lifts the oval cup by its earlike handles and drinks of the soupy venison-and-taro-root stew. She nibbles strips of ox meat threaded on bamboo skewers. Using chopsticks, she tears pheasant meat from the bone. The pheasant is delicious—seasoned with honey and soy sauce, just as she likes it. She lifts the lid from a cup and sips warm beer.

Lady Dai sighs in contentment as a quintet of musicians strikes up a lively folk song, plucking zithers and blowing mouth organs. Dancers gracefully twirl, bend, and dip their bodies. Their long silk sleeves swirl and flutter like flying birds. Singers add words to the music:

> *For the beauty and the music are so enchanting,*
> *The beholder, delighted, forgets that he must go.*
> *Tighten the zither's strings and smite them in unison!*
> *Strike the bells until the bell-stand rocks!*

If the souls of the Marquis of Dai, Lady Dai, and their son were to be comfortable in their underground homes, they would need amenities—especially food, dishes, servants, and entertainment.

The elaborate dinner party set up for Lady Dai in the north compartment of her burial chamber showed a scene she must have often enjoyed: appetizing delicacies presented on splendid lacquerware in a festive atmosphere of melody and movement.

An Everlasting Feast

The three storage compartments of Lady Dai's burial chamber were filled with food: grains, vegetables, fruits, meat, poultry, fish, spices, sauces, and

This banquet scene was set up in the north compartment, above Lady Dai's head. On the left side is an area for her soul to sit on a silk couch with a silk pillow. A lacquer screen stands behind the couch, and a tray of lacquer dishes with food lies in front of it. On the right side of the compartment are wooden figurines of entertainers and servants.
HUNAN PROVINCIAL MUSEUM

Well-preserved samples of fruits and seeds from Lady Dai's tomb show some of the foods eaten in the early Han dynasty. HUNAN PROVINCIAL MUSEUM

Foods for a Mother and Son
Foods found in the tombs of Lady Dai and her son reveal the variety and richness of the aristocratic Han diet.

Grains: rice, millet, wheat, barley, hemp seeds

Vegetables: soybeans, red beans, bamboo shoots, lotus roots, ginger roots, taro, mustard seeds, mallow, Chinese cabbage, amaranth

Fruits: Chinese pears, jujubes, plums, peaches, red bayberries, melons

Meats: hare, dog, pig, deer, ox, sheep

Birds: goose, duck, chicken, pheasant, crane, pigeon, quail, partridge, owl, magpie, sparrow eggs

Fish: carp, goldfish, catfish, bream, perch

Seasonings: salt, sugar, honey, soy sauce, salty bean sauce, vinegar, cinnamon bark, Sichuan pepper, magnolia buds, galangal

Beverages: fruit juices; alcoholic drinks made from rice, wheat, and millet

beverages. The conditions that helped preserve Lady Dai's body also preserved the food stored in her tomb. Being able to see, touch, and smell actual food prepared almost 2,200 years ago made real what researchers had only been able to read about in ancient descriptions, study in ancient paintings, or discern from stone carvings.

Information written on bamboo strips revealed even more, describing the seasonings, cooking methods, and preserving processes of the time. Researchers knew that the most common entrée in Han cuisine was a stew called *geng*, which was eaten by both wealthy and poor families. *Geng* could be made of many different combinations of grains, vegetables, meat, and fish. The bamboo strips in Lady Dai's tomb listed specific combinations of ingredients, such as beef and rice, chicken and gourd, pork and turnip, or venison with salted fish and bamboo shoots.

Nine small boxes containing cosmetics, two powder puffs, a wig, and four combs were found in the bottom layer of this lacquer box. The top layer held three pairs of gloves, a scarf, a belt, and an embroidered mirror case—all made of silk.
HUNAN PROVINCIAL MUSEUM

Lavish Lacquerware

In Han times the wealthy dined from lacquer dishes. The poor ate from dishes made of wood, pottery, or bamboo. As a symbol of Lady Dai's wealth and status, 184 pieces of lacquerware were buried in her tomb. Her husband and son had even more.

What is lacquer? It starts as sap inside a tree, chiefly the species *Toxicodendron vernicifluum,* also called the Chinese lacquer tree. The sap's main component is urushiol, which is the substance in poison ivy that produces an intensely itchy rash for many people. Despite this toxicity, ancient Chinese figured out how to make lacquer at least seven thousand years ago. They used it for cooking utensils, dishes, furniture, storage boxes, weapon accessories, musical instruments, vases, and even coffins.

Making lacquerware requires a great deal of labor. For the Mawangdui pieces, sap was collected from trees and then exposed to oxygen in a moist environment. This caused the sap to polymerize (undergo a chemical reaction in which small molecules bond together to form larger molecules) and transform into lacquer. Artisans applied multiple thin coats of lacquer to a core of wood, clay, fabric, or bamboo, letting each layer dry before applying the next. They then painted the object with colored lacquer or tung oil (an oil from nuts of the tung tree that hardens into a waterproof coating). A few special objects, such as Lady Dai's cosmetic containers, were decorated with gold leaf. Most were labeled with inscriptions carved with a needle: "Household of the Marquis of Dai," "Please eat the food," or "Please drink the wine."

The finished lacquerware was elegant: glossy and brilliantly colored, with swirling designs that ranged from delicate to bold. It was also as practical as it was beautiful. A natural plastic, lacquer resists damage by water, heat, bacteria, termites, acids, and alkalis. Hidden within her tomb, Lady Dai's lacquerware endured for two millennia in splendid condition.

Servants Standing By

Besides the attendants and entertainers at her banquet, Lady Dai had wooden servants in other parts of her underground home. Three dozen small figurines crudely carved of peach wood rested on her innermost coffin, perhaps to protect her from evil spirits. Larger figurines in the north, east, and south compartments had carved noses; lips painted red; and eyes, eyebrows, and various hairstyles painted in black. Most wore painted clothing, but some were garbed in actual silk gowns. Altogether, Lady Dai had 162 wooden servants available to tend to her needs in the afterlife.

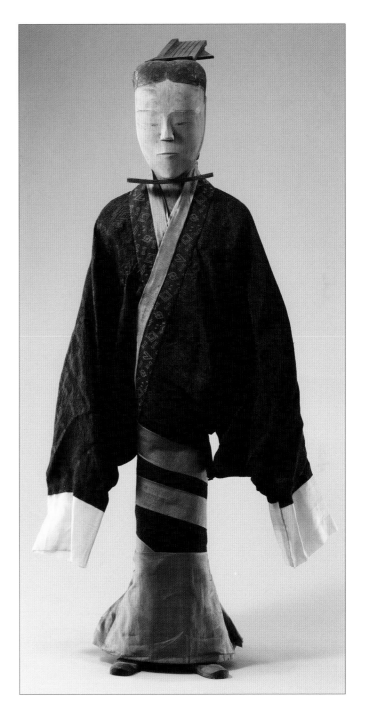

This "man with a hat" (*guanren*) likely represents a head steward in charge of Lady Dai's household matters. He wears a silk robe and stands 31 inches (79 centimeters) tall. HUNAN PROVINCIAL MUSEUM

Mingqi, or spirit objects, were wooden or clay models designed to be buried in tombs. They included figurines of servants, soldiers, and entertainers, as well as models of ceremonial vessels, musical instruments, and coins. (Lady Dai's tomb contained more than one hundred thousand clay coins.) Later in the Han dynasty, *mingqi* expanded to include pottery models of houses, stoves, wells, granaries, and farm animals in stalls. *Mingqi* were supposed to resemble their real counterparts but not be functional: they might be missing components or be made of inferior materials, or their sizes and proportions might be distorted. Although *mingqi* were unusable to the living, they were thought to be very real necessities for the souls of the dead.

Music for the Soul

Musical instruments offered melodies for Xin Zhui's soul in her underground home. Some were made just for burial and were unplayable. These replicas included not only the miniature instruments provided for the wooden musicians at Lady Dai's dinner party but also larger models. One funerary replica was a *yu* mouth organ composed of a wooden mouthpiece with vertical bamboo pipes arranged in rows. Although it looked realistic, it could not be played because the mouthpiece had no blow hole and the pipes had no air holes. The son's tomb had small-scale wooden models that represented bronze bells and stone chimes.

In addition to these replicas, genuine, full-size musical instruments were buried in the tombs. They revealed lost secrets of ancient Chinese music to modern-day researchers.

The *se* zither found in Lady Dai's burial chamber was the first complete, well-preserved *se* of the early Han dynasty ever recovered. A player would have knelt behind the large wooden instrument (nearly as wide as a standard piano keyboard) and plucked its twenty-five silk strings with the thumb and index finger of both hands. The strings were tuned by sliding the bridges underneath them. A similar *se* was buried with the son.

Another genuine instrument found in the son's tomb was a wooden *qin* zither, the first of its kind to be discovered. It had scratch marks—evidence that it had been played, perhaps by the son himself. The *qin* had seven silk strings that were tuned by turning pegs to loosen or tighten them. It could be played across one's lap. The *qin* was the favorite instrument of scholars, who played it to nurture and express inner calm.

During Xin Zhui's time, music and dancing were valued for more than just recreation. Confucian philosophers valued music for its power to foster virtue and proper behavior. They believed that good government was reflected in ceremonial music that sounded harmonious, peaceful, and orderly.

The entertainers in the banquet scene included these five figurines of musicians—three with *se* zithers and two with *yu* mouth organs—as well as four singers and four dancers.

The tomb of Lady Dai's son contained a board game called *liubo*, which was very popular during the Han dynasty. HUNAN PROVINCIAL MUSEUM

A Game for Fun and Fortune

Like people everywhere across time, people in ancient China loved playing games. One of the most popular chess games during the Han dynasty was *liubo*. Sculptures and pictures from other tombs show players enjoying rousing games of *liubo,* their body postures animated and their facial expressions gleeful (for winners) or dismayed (for losers).

Lady Dai's son was apparently an avid player, because a set of *liubo* equipment was found in his tomb. The most complete set yet discovered, it included a square wooden game board with pathways, black and white ivory playing pieces, ivory counting rods, and a wooden die. The die had eighteen sides, which were labeled with the numerals 1 to 16, the word *jiao* (a favorable move), and the word *qiwei* (an unfavorable move).

During the Han dynasty everyone from emperors to commoners, both men and women, played variations of the game. Two players would take turns throwing the die and moving their playing pieces, trying to block their opponent. Unfortunately, the exact rules of the game have been lost.

While *liubo* was a game that was associated with gambling, it also aided in divination. People used the board, rods, and moves to predict future events regarding marriage, travel, disease, and death.

With stockpiles of food, elegant dishes, musical instruments, a popular game, and servants galore, the souls of Lady Dai and her family were equipped to enjoy sumptuous banquets and carefree days in their underground homes. As promised in the ancient Chinese poem "Summons of the Soul,"

> All your household have come to do you honour; all kinds
>   of good foods are ready. . . .
> Bitter, salt, sour, hot and sweet: there are dishes of
>   all flavours. . . .
> Before the dainties have left the tables, girl musicians
>   take up their places.
> They set up the bells and fasten the drums and sing
>   the latest songs. . . .
> Pipes and zither rise in wild harmonies, the sounding drums
>   thunderously roll.

5

Lady Dai's Silk Treasures

A sound like pattering rain fills Lady Dai's ears as pale silkworms munch mulberry leaves on the tray in front of her. She spreads fresh leaves for them—leaves that she plucked this morning, then washed, dried, and chopped. She sighs in weariness. For the last three weeks she has constantly tended these delicate creatures, keeping them warm, dry, and clean—and feeding them day and night. But soon they will stop eating. Then each tiny silkworm will weave a cocoon around itself, secreting a sticky liquid as it gyrates its head in a figure eight. This process is magic to Lady Dai, no matter how many times she sees it.

Shields of Silk

Not only is silk stronger than steel, it also can stretch without breaking. Chinese and Mongolian soldiers wore silk under their leather or metal armor for protection. Arrows rip flesh when they are pulled out. However, if a soldier wore silk, an arrow would enter the body but not tear through the silk. When the silk was carefully tugged, the arrow would emerge cleanly.

In the 1880s in Arizona, a physician named George E. Goodfellow witnessed similar effects in gunfights. In three cases, a bullet that should have gone all the way through a man's body was stopped by his silk handkerchief.

Silk even protects modern soldiers. In 2011 the US military began issuing silk undershorts to soldiers in Afghanistan to keep sand and other small particles out of wounds caused by explosives.

Who would have guessed that the cocoon of a caterpillar could be transformed into a luxurious fabric—one that is delicate enough to make a transparent gown, yet strong enough to resist being punctured by an arrow?

For more than two thousand years, only the Chinese knew the secrets to making silk. They perfected the art of raising silkworms and unraveling each cocoon into a single, unbroken thread. From the thread, they wove a soft, glossy, airy cloth that was the height of luxury in the ancient world.

When people from other countries encountered silk, they were fascinated. Wealthy citizens of the Roman Empire clamored for the wondrous material and paid a pound of gold for a pound of silk. They bought so much that Roman leaders complained about how much money flowed eastward for the fabric.

Within China, silk was so valuable that it was used as money, as part of the salary of officials, and as gifts from the emperor to other nations. During the Han dynasty, its popularity soared. Not only did the powerful and wealthy wear silk, but they also dressed their servants, entertainers, and guests in silk. Even soldiers wore silk as part of their armor. The prized fabric hung in houses, carriages, and boats. Lavish quantities of silk were used in funerals and burials for members of aristocratic families—families like Lady Dai's.

Surrounded by Silk

In life Lady Dai would have dressed in fine silk robes—possibly of her own making. Even though she was a wealthy woman, she most likely knew how to make silk. Producing silk was a valued and valuable industry in ancient

China, with women participating from all social classes—from the palace to the fields. The activities of sericulture (breeding silkworms), weaving, and sewing were considered proper and virtuous. Even if a woman did not need to earn money, she earned a good reputation by pursuing these activities.

In death Lady Dai was literally surrounded by silk—evidence of her privileged status. After she died mourners cocooned her body in twenty layers of silk clothing. They tied nine silk bands around the bundle, placed it inside a silk-lined coffin, and covered it with two padded silk quilts. The coffin was decorated on the outside with silk brocade and embroidered silk and tied with two more silk bands.

The silk-wrapped body of Lady Dai lay within this silk-decorated coffin. Feathers and strips of silk were glued onto thin silk, which was then pasted onto the lid and the four sides of the coffin. Strips of embroidered silk formed an outer border.

Lady Dai was well supplied with silk in other parts of her burial chamber as well. Bamboo cases contained abundant silk clothing (gowns, robes, skirts, gloves, socks, shoes, and belts), along with forty-six rolls of the precious fabric. Brightening her underground home were elegant silk curtains and pillows, as well as silk coverings for her bronze mirror, cosmetic boxes, and musical instruments.

The Mysterious *Feiyi*

The most valuable of Lady Dai's treasures is an elaborate silk painting called a *feiyi*, meaning "flying garment." Shaped like a T and measuring almost 6 feet 9 inches (205 centimeters) long, it covered the length of the innermost coffin. When archaeologists discovered the *feiyi*, they were amazed. They had read about but never seen such a painting. It was the first *feiyi* ever found.

But the archaeologists' excitement soon turned to concern. How could they recover the *feiyi* without damaging it? Being so old, it was fragile; they could not just pick it up. So they whittled strips of bamboo, polishing away any rough edges. Using these smooth, flexible tools, they painstakingly peeled the *feiyi* off the lid of Lady Dai's coffin. As they progressed, they rolled the *feiyi* around a large paper tube. At last they could examine the intricate painting in detail.

In the center is a portrait of Lady Dai, dressed in a long, loose gown with

This T-shaped silk painting *(feiyi)* lay facedown on the lid of the innermost coffin. The upper section represents heaven, the middle section depicts earthly life, and the lower section represents the underworld. HUNAN PROVINCIAL MUSEUM

This close-up of Lady Dai (center) is from the lower middle section of the *feiyi*. Experts wonder if it portrays her in her earthly life or in the afterlife, possibly on her journey to paradise or heaven.

HUNAN PROVINCIAL MUSEUM

swirled decorations. She is leaning on a walking stick with three female servants standing behind her and two male servants kneeling in front of her. Above and below them are other human figures, deities, mythological beasts, and symbols such as the sun and moon.

The *feiyi* has inspired many different interpretations of its purpose. Why was this silk painting lying on top of the coffin? What was its function?

A few researchers have wondered if the *feiyi* was used in the "summoning the soul" ritual—the last attempt to keep the *hun* soul from wandering away forever.

Some experts believe the *feiyi* was hung at the house next to the coffin before burial. The painting identified the body—perhaps to remind mourners of Lady Dai or to help her soul recognize her body if it returned.

One of forty pieces of embroidered silk found in Lady Dai's tomb. The chain-stitch embroidery displays a "long life" *(changshou)* pattern of swirling clouds. HUNAN PROVINCIAL MUSEUM

Many experts believe the *feiyi* was carried like a banner ahead of the coffins in the funeral procession to the grave. There it was buried facedown on top of the innermost coffin.

Others believe it was simply a shroud to cover the dead before the funeral and then to cover the coffin.

Even more mysterious than the *feiyi's* purpose is its meaning. What do the images on Lady Dai's banner represent? Most researchers agree that the banner shows three worlds: the heavenly realm, the earthly realm, and the underworld.

But beyond these major themes, experts disagree on how to interpret the images. The paintings might show Lady Dai in the afterlife. Perhaps they depict the journey of her soul to paradise or to heaven. The *feiyi* could be a type of road map to guide the way. Or maybe it represents a combination of different beliefs about the spiritual world and the afterlife.

Revelations in Silk

Silk—unlike hardier materials such as stone, bronze, or fired clay—rarely survives being stashed in a tomb for thousands of years. Much of what we used to know about the history of Chinese silk came from scarce fragments of the cloth or written descriptions.

Then came the discoveries at Mawangdui. Although the silk clothing around Lady Dai's body had rotted from soaking in the coffin liquid, the silks stored in the rest of her burial chamber were in wonderful condition. They gave researchers the opportunity to examine firsthand the skill and creativity of ancient artisans.

Some of the silks had intricate patterns woven into them. Many were further decorated with embroidery, painting, or block printing. More than twenty different dyes created a kaleidoscope of colors. The silks buried with Lady Dai provide clear evidence of how advanced ancient China was in sericulture, weaving technology, textile design, dyeing, embroidery, and other decorative techniques.

When archaeologists opened the tomb of Lady Dai's son, they discovered more silk treasures—another *feiyi*, clothing, fabric, and furnishings—and also, to their surprise, an extraordinary trove that would change their understanding of early imperial China.

6

Library of Silk and Bamboo

*L*ady Dai is proud of her son. He is a general, responsible for defending the southern border of the Changsha Kingdom. But she is also worried for him. Just over the boundary lies the land of the Nanyue tribes, whose king attacked Changsha ten years ago. Ever since, soldiers on both sides of the border have nervously watched each other, wondering when the next conflict will erupt.

Lady Dai sees how the pressure weighs on her son. She watches as he pulls out a map and a book on military strategy. He studies where the mountains and rivers lie and ponders how best to use the terrain to trap and defeat the enemy. He fixes every detail in his mind, because when the time for battle comes, he must be ready.

Every time her son goes to war, Lady Dai wonders if she will see him again.

A dark lacquer box lay in the east compartment of the son's burial chamber, resting among lacquer dishes. Its undecorated exterior gave no hint of the treasure hidden within. When archaeologists lifted the lid, they found numerous folded rectangles of silk, two lengths of silk wrapped around a stick, and two rolls of bamboo and wooden strips. The silks and strips were covered with writing. These were books and documents—including the oldest and largest cache of silk books discovered in China. In that single box were fifty manuscripts consisting of over one hundred thousand characters (words). Many contained content that no one had read for one to two thousand years. Scholars around the world were excited, as they had long assumed the material was lost—destroyed in fires or wars, or through decay.

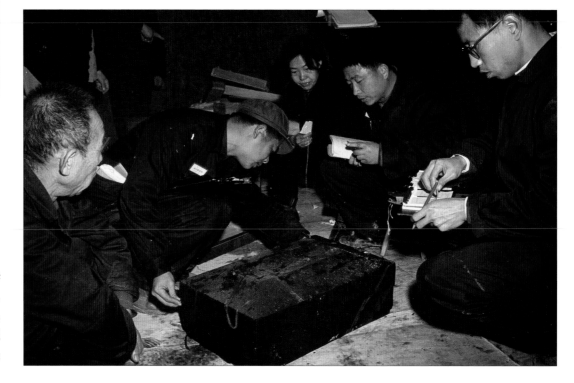

This lacquer box was found in the son's tomb. It contained maps, charts, and long-lost books on medicine, philosophy, divination, history, and politics. Hunan Provincial Museum

Words on Bamboo and Silk

The first books in China were written on narrow strips of bamboo and wood. Each narrow strip had one column of characters written in ink with a brush. If the writer made a mistake, he could erase it by shaving it off with a knife. The strips were tied together and then either rolled up or folded accordion-style.

Bamboo and wood provided a smooth surface for writing, and their supply was plentiful. However, the narrow strips offered limited writing space. When the bindings broke or rotted, the strips often fell out of order or were lost. Bulky, heavy books were also difficult to store and carry. One Han dynasty official is said to have written a report of thirty thousand to forty thousand words; the bundle of three thousand strips required two men to carry it to the emperor.

Silk was the next new writing material, overlapping bamboo and wood for about one thousand years. Silk possessed many fine qualities for writing purposes. Long books could be written on a single piece, cut at whatever length was needed. Large sheets of silk were good for paintings, maps, charts, and diagrams. Silk was also lightweight and easy to roll up or fold, so it was convenient to carry and store. Because silk was so expensive, it was reserved for classical literature, valued topics such as medicine and divination, sacred texts, and imperial documents.

Although silk documents were meant to be permanent records, the silk itself usually rotted away over time, and the information disappeared with it. In addition, untold numbers of books were destroyed in political upheavals—burned, stolen, and even cut up to make satchels or tents.

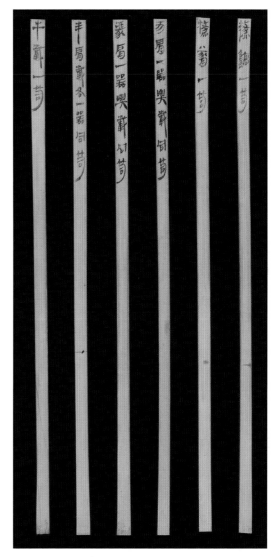

An inventory of objects that were to be buried in Lady Dai's tomb was written on 312 bamboo strips. (The actual objects found in her tomb varied slightly from the planned inventory.) These strips list meat from various animals.
Hunan Provincial Museum

Censorship played a role as well. In 213 BCE China's first emperor confiscated and burned historical and philosophical books that could be used to criticize him.

With such threats to their very existence, the survival of numerous books—especially silk books—at Mawangdui is extremely significant. Their information filled gaps in modern knowledge of early China and expanded our understanding of life and thought in those times.

How to Predict the Future

The ancient Chinese noticed that regular patterns occurred in nature: night followed day; the seasons changed; living things grew, then declined and died. But they also observed that breaks in the normal patterns occurred, sometimes bringing disasters such as earthquakes, floods, or droughts. People believed that if they lived in harmony with the cosmos, they would achieve success and avoid misfortune. This desire motivated them to study nature systematically, searching for omens that could be used to foretell events in their lives.

In the son's library were handbooks of divination based on observations of the position and appearance of celestial bodies. *Wuxing zhan (Divination by Five Stars)* reports data on the movements of the planets Mercury, Venus, Mars, Jupiter, and Saturn, including surprisingly accurate calculations of the time each takes to make a complete orbit around the sun. *Tianwen qixiang zazhan (Miscellaneous Divination by Astrology or Meteorology)* displays twenty-nine drawings of comets, showing various tail shapes.

Other texts instruct the reader in interpreting cloud shapes, wind

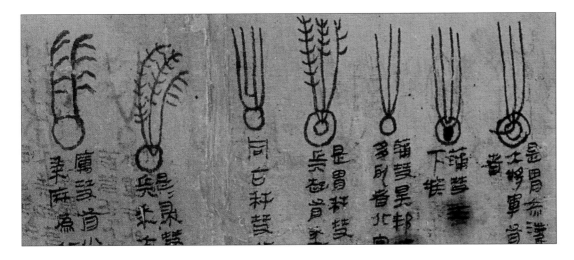

These drawings of comets with tails of various shapes come from the book *Miscellaneous Divination by Astrology and Meteorology.*
HUNAN PROVINCIAL MUSEUM

patterns, mirages, mists, and rainbows. People used these and other forms of divination to answer questions about the future: Will an action succeed? Will rain come? Will a child be born? Should troops be mobilized? Unusual events such as comets, earthquakes, and eclipses were interpreted as warnings that a ruler was misusing power.

How to Rule an Empire

For five hundred years (722–221 BCE), China suffered war after war as feudal states competed with each other. During this turbulent period, rulers of the various states wanted to know how to maintain their power, as well as how to establish peace and prosperity. Philosophers offered many different solutions. One influential philosophy was a branch of Daoism called Huang-Lao, which remained popular well into the Han dynasty. Han Wendi, the emperor who reigned from 180 BCE to 157 BCE—during the lifetimes of Lady Dai and her son—favored this approach to ruling the empire.

This silk fragment is part of the book *Prescriptions for Fifty-two Ailments,* which lists 283 medical, herbal, and magical treatments. Composed of nearly ten thousand words, it is the longest of the medical books found in the son's tomb.

Historical records mention Huang-Lao Daoism briefly, but texts detailing the philosophy had disappeared. For two thousand years no one knew what its actual tenets were—until the discovery at Mawangdui of two copies of the main Daoist text, *Laozi (The Canon),* and four supplementary texts.

These texts advocate applying a Daoist approach to government. To govern successfully, a ruler must deeply understand the order of nature and act in harmony with it. A true ruler is trustworthy, unbiased, and not self-centered; he exemplifies a life of simplicity and frugality. A true ruler does not burden people with harsh laws and high taxes. He establishes a government that is stable and orderly, so people know what to expect.

How to Cure an Ailment

Until the Mawangdui excavations the oldest known Chinese medical book was *Huangdi neijing (The Yellow Emperor's Inner Classic).* But the fourteen texts hidden in the son's tomb were even older and changed how scholars viewed ancient Chinese medical theory and practice. The texts represent a transitional stage between two different ways of explaining illness. In the older view people believed that disease resulted from causes outside the body, such as demons, insects, or climate conditions. In the new theory illness stemmed from problems of *qi* circulation within the body. *Qi* was believed to be the mysterious life force that permeates the natural world, including the human body.

The longest of the medical texts, *Wushier bingfang (Prescriptions for Fifty-two Ailments),* describes how to treat wounds, warts, boils, abscesses, hemorrhoids, poisoning, and animal bites by using either magical rituals or

This replica of the "Drawings of Guiding and Pulling" chart shows breathing and stretching exercises to improve one's health. Hunan Provincial Museum

medicine. To cure a wart, seven different remedies are given. One remedy involves performing a ritual dance while chanting and rubbing the wart with dirt clods. Another says to touch the wart with the burning tip of a cord made of cattail leaves.

Exercise was valued in ancient China, much as it is today. An exercise chart called "*Daoyin tu* (Drawings of Guiding and Pulling)" portrays forty-four human figures in various poses. Some of these poses imitate animals, including the grasshopper, crane, eagle, bear, dragon, and monkey. Captions recommend using certain positions for specific ailments, such as indigestion, fever, or headaches. The pose captioned "Monkey Bawling to Pull Internal Hotness" shows a man standing with clenched fists at his waist, his mouth open, perhaps to blow out fire *qi*, which was believed to cause illness.

This silk garrison map represents the border area between the Changsha and Nanyue kingdoms, with south at the top. With symbols indicating the location of military troops and facilities, it shows the defense strategy set up in Changsha after it was invaded by Nanyue. HUNAN PROVINCIAL MUSEUM

How to Plan for War

Historical documents speak of maps in ancient China, but all the actual maps had disappeared—until three silk maps were discovered in the son's lacquer box. The maps had fallen apart along their fold lines, but the information preserved on them is evidence of the high level of skill of early Chinese cartographers.

The maps, along with thirty-eight weapons and a black military cap, are clues that Lady Dai's son had been an officer of high rank, perhaps a general. The garrison map would have been essential to him because it details Changsha's defense strategy after neighboring Nanyue attacked in 181 BCE. Before planning a campaign, the commander had to know the terrain of the area: Where were the mountains and rivers, and where should troops cross them? Where could the enemy hide? How big were the cities, and which could be used as fortresses? How long were the routes? Commanders depended on maps to answer these questions.

The Mawangdui maps use various symbols and colors to depict rivers (including size and direction of water flow), mountains (including slope and height), positions of military troops and buildings, and cities and villages of civilians. The maps display information gained by using advanced methods of mathematics. Also noteworthy is their representation of actual distances through the use of scale.

Widespread use of sophisticated maps accurately made to

scale put China ahead in cartography compared to other ancient civilizations, including Greece and Rome.

The Hidden Library

During the time of Lady Dai and her family, scholars commonly had personal libraries for their own reading and studying. They even traveled with their libraries, as the son might have done, his books and maps packed conveniently in their lacquer box. Some scholars had so many books of bamboo strips that they needed carts to transport them, inspiring the popular Chinese saying that to be well educated, a person needs to have read five cartloads of books.

Lady Dai's son died relatively young, leading experts to wonder if he died in battle. His library was buried in his tomb with him and was therefore spared the fate of most other ancient books. Above ground, emperors gained and lost power, wars raged, and earthquakes and floods wreaked havoc. Centuries marched by, during which imperial libraries were set ablaze a dozen times, reducing thousands of books to ashes. Of the nearly six hundred titles listed in the first-century catalog of the Han imperial library, the vast majority have disappeared. Today, fewer than one hundred have been recovered as complete or partial manuscripts.

The fifty books preserved in the son's library were greeted with excitement by scholars around the globe. The rediscovered texts brought knowledge and insights from ancient writers to modern readers, allowing us to hear two-thousand-year-old thoughts on questions that still concern us today: how to govern a nation, how to treat illness, and how to live in harmony with the world around us.

Multiple Uses for Maps
In addition to using maps for warfare, the ancient Chinese employed maps for many other purposes. Administrators studied them to know the boundaries of their territories, to manage water supply projects, and to regulate agriculture and mining. Planners consulted them to select auspicious building sites. Rulers learned their domain's geography and obtained maps of lands they conquered. People also used maps for religious purposes: to arrange equipment for rituals, to interpret astrological signs, and as talismans against evil spirits. Maps were buried in tombs, according to some experts, to show the person's former domain and power.

Conclusion

Time Capsule of Mawangdui

The three tombs of Mawangdui preserved and revealed in exquisite detail the lifestyle of a privileged and wealthy family in the early Han dynasty.

Thanks to this incredible time capsule, we know what Lady Dai ate and what she wore. We can picture her leaning back against a pillow while listening to her favorite music. We can examine the books her son read and guess at how he played his favorite game. We can view the signature seals her husband pressed onto official documents to identify his title and position.

We can also ponder the thoughts and beliefs of people who lived more than two thousand years ago. We in the twenty-first century CE can recognize that those in the third century BCE were not so different from us.

We enjoy good food, music, dancing, and games. So did they.

They watched the stars and planets, mapped their territories, and created works of art. So do we.

We get sick, take medicines, and when the time comes, bury our dead. So did they.

They wondered about the nature of the universe, how people should behave, what would happen in their lives, and what awaited them in the afterlife. So do we.

By learning about people of the past, we learn about ourselves in the present. In some aspects our lives differ from theirs. But in many aspects we are very much the same—in our questions, in our hopes, and in our desire to understand the world and our place within it.

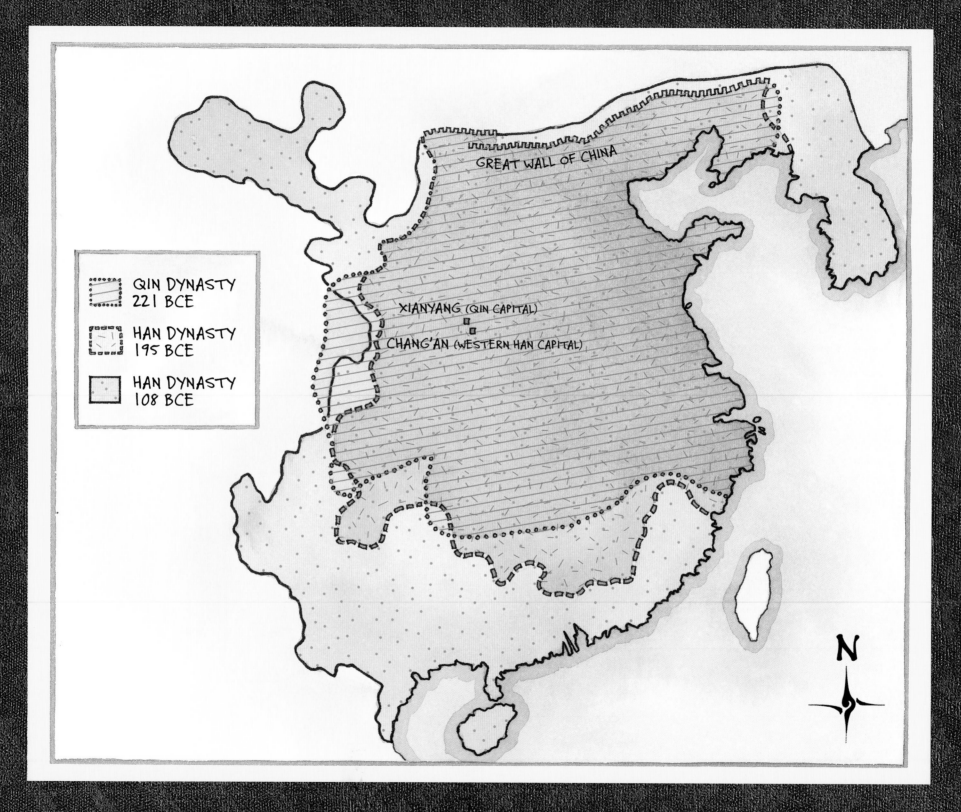

GREAT WALL OF CHINA

QIN DYNASTY
221 BCE

HAN DYNASTY
195 BCE

HAN DYNASTY
108 BCE

XIANYANG (QIN CAPITAL)

CHANG'AN (WESTERN HAN CAPITAL)

N

Historical Note
Legacy of the Qin and Han Dynasties

Qin Shihuangdi: The Conqueror

Over five centuries of war, more than one hundred major states were whittled down to seven. Finally the state of Qin conquered its six rivals, and in 221 BCE the king of Qin crowned himself Shihuangdi (First Awe-Inspiring Emperor). For the first time China was a unified empire under one ruler.

Over the millennia many people have said that Shihuangdi was a brutal tyrant who burned books and buried scholars alive. One contemporary remarked, "He killed men as though he thought he could never finish, he punished men as though he were afraid he would never get around to them all." But in recent years historians question whether the portrayal stems from Han critics exaggerating how bad the first emperor was in order to boost the image of the later Han dynasty.

History is clear, however, that Shihuangdi created a unified empire and began forging a new national identity and common culture that defined what it meant to be Chinese. The challenge was how to convert the various states—which had their own governments, laws, and traditions—into a single, cohesive nation.

Lady Dai and her family lived during a pivotal time in China's history. They witnessed the turbulent birth and early development of the Chinese empire.

To set up the authority of the central government with himself as the supreme ruler, Shihuangdi eliminated individual kingdoms. Instead, he divided the empire into commanderies run by appointed officials. The old kings and powerful families were moved to the capital, Xianyang, away from their former spheres of influence. Shihuangdi also conquered new territories and moved approximately two million people to settle these areas, further intermixing the population.

To create a unified culture across the empire, Shihuangdi established a single written language so people in different regions could all read the same texts (even if they spoke different dialects). To eliminate confusion arising from separate measurement systems, Shihuangdi instituted one set of weights and measures. A round coin with a square hole in the center replaced coins of other shapes. A single code of law was adopted—a strict code with severe physical punishments for both the criminal and the criminal's family.

To connect and defend the empire, Shihuangdi launched massive construction projects. The Great Wall expanded on existing walls and stretched over 3,100 miles (5,000 kilometers) to protect China from raids by northern tribes. More than 5,200 miles (8,400 kilometers) of highways branched outward from the capital, facilitating travel, communication, and transportation of goods.

Shihuangdi succeeded in creating a unified empire, but he failed at winning people's hearts. Two scholars who fled from his service concluded, "The emperor, never hearing his faults condemned, is growing prouder and prouder while those below cringe in fear and try to please him with flattery

Li Cang is probably in his twenties during this period, perhaps working on a construction project and/or serving as a minor official. Meanwhile, Xin Zhui is born during Shihuangdi's reign.

and lies." So many drastic changes over so short a time (eleven years) was too much for people to accept. After Shihuangdi died and his son assumed the throne, rebellions broke out and chaos ensued.

Han Gaozu: The Consolidator

Battles for power raged until one man emerged as victor. Born a peasant, Liu Bang became a village official, a rebel, a governor, a military leader, and then king of the Han territory in 206 BCE. He was famous for capturing the Qin capital but not plundering it, instead saying to its citizens, "For a long time you have suffered beneath the harsh laws of Qin. . . . I have come only to save you from further harm, not to exploit or tyrannize over you." After defeating his chief rival, Xiang Yu, Liu Bang was crowned emperor in 202 BCE, founding the Han dynasty. He is remembered by the title Gaozu (High Ancestor) or Gaodi (High Emperor).

Like Shihuangdi, Gaozu won the empire through military victories and then faced the challenge of governing it. As one of his advisers, Lu Jia, pointed out: "Your Majesty may have won it [the empire] on horseback, but can you rule it on horseback?" Lu Jia argued that the Qin dynasty had fallen because it had not adapted its methods from waging war to establishing a stable, well-functioning empire. After centuries of war the empire needed to be stabilized politically and economically, and the people needed to recover and resume normal lives. How could Gaozu succeed where Shihuangdi had failed?

Gaozu possessed personality traits that helped him as emperor. Since he was born a peasant, he understood the needs of commoners and governed with their interests in mind. He won respect for his moral integrity and for

Emperors and Their Many Names
Chinese emperors had multiple names. Each started with a name given at birth, such as Liu Bang (family name followed by personal name). While he was emperor it was forbidden to speak or write his given name, so he was addressed as Shang (The Superior One) or by other indirect references to his imperial position.

After an emperor died he was given a title describing him or his reign, such as Gaozu (High Ancestor) or Wudi (Military Emperor). Emperors in different dynasties sometimes had the same posthumous title; to avoid confusion, the dynasty when the emperor reigned is also indicated. For example, Han Gaodi was Gaodi (High Emperor) of the Han dynasty.

being tolerant, fair, and merciful. He secured the loyalty of key supporters by recognizing their strengths, following their advice, and rewarding them with land and prestigious positions.

Gaozu adopted the basic government structure set up by Shihuangdi, but he changed the legal code so that people were treated more humanely. He put out a call for men of merit to be recommended for administrative positions. He divided the west into fourteen commanderies under his control, and the east into ten kingdoms ruled by his allies (nine of whom were soon replaced by Gaozu's relatives).

One of the new kingdoms was Changsha, a sparsely populated territory that served as a strategic military outpost against the southern tribes. Gaozu made one of his supporters the king of Changsha, and for five generations (until 157 BCE) it remained the only kingdom not ruled by a relative of the emperor. Li Cang was appointed the first chancellor and served under four of Changsha's kings.

After only seven years as emperor, Gaozu died in 195 BCE of an arrow wound sustained in battle. His oldest son, Liu Ying, called Huidi (Benevolent Emperor), and his widow, Lü Hou, headed the empire until 180 BCE. Then Gaozu's fifth son, Liu Heng, was chosen to be the next emperor. He is known as Wendi (Civil Emperor).

Han Wendi: The Nurturer

Wendi is praised for being a virtuous, frugal, and compassionate ruler who brought stability and prosperity to the empire during his reign of twenty-three years. He strengthened the central government and reduced the power

Li Cang helps vanquish the enemy Gaozu was fighting when he died, for which he is awarded the title Marquis of Dai and its fiefdom. As his wife, Xin Zhui becomes the Marquise (or Marchioness) of Dai, or, as she is frequently called today, Lady Dai. Li Cang dies in 186 BCE. Five years later, Changsha is attacked by the southern kingdom of Nanyue.

of individual kingdoms. The economy grew so well that he lowered and then eliminated the tax on farmers' crops. He gave food to the poor. He abolished some of the worst physical punishments, arguing that "if the laws are just, the people will be obedient."

Wendi dressed simply. He avoided lavishness in the palaces and in preparations for his tomb. A conscientious emperor, he conducted his life to serve as a good example to all, saying, "I have risen early and retired late, labouring for the sake of the empire and taking thought for the people: for them I have been filled with concern and unrest, and their troubles have not left my mind for a single day."

After Wendi's death in 157 BCE, his son Liu Qi became emperor. Remembered as Jingdi (Admirable Emperor), he continued building up the central government by reducing the size and independence of individual kingdoms. In protest, seven kings staged a revolt, but they were defeated. The economy continued to grow, and food was abundant. However, major changes took place when Jingdi's sixteen-year-old son, Liu Che, known as Wudi (Military Emperor), assumed the throne in 141 BCE.

Han Wudi: The Expansionist

In his fifty-four years as emperor, Wudi brought China to a peak of power. The borders expanded north, east, south, and west into modern-day Mongolia, Korea, Vietnam, and Central Asia, adding approximately 1.6 million square miles (4.1 million square kilometers) and several million people to the empire. Trade along the Silk Road from China to the Roman Empire greatly increased. The Imperial Academy was established, where boys

Li Cang and Xin Zhui's son serves as a general on Changsha's southern border with Nanyue. He dies in 168 BCE, perhaps in battle. Ten years later, Xin Zhui suffers a fatal heart attack. Her tomb, and that of her son, are more lavishly furnished than Li Cang's, likely reflecting the family's greater wealth under Wendi's rule—yet both tombs still obey Wendi's order forbidding the burial of jade, gold, silver, and bronze in tombs.

aged fourteen to seventeen studied to become government officials. Four new palaces were built and furnished luxuriously in Chang'an, the capital.

But Wudi's ambitious expansion and extravagance were costly. The imperial treasury was drained, even though the government raised taxes and controlled prices. Agriculture suffered, and many peasants had to sell their land to pay their taxes. The overextended empire began declining.

After Wudi's death in 87 BCE, the remaining emperors of what is now called the Western Han dynasty instituted reforms to recover from Wudi's excesses. But the empire never regained its former strength and collapsed in 9 CE. Wang Mang, a high official, tried to found a new dynasty but failed. A descendant of Jingdi then reclaimed the empire for the Liu family and in 25 CE started the Eastern Han dynasty (so named because the capital was moved from Chang'an in the west to Luoyang in the east), which lasted until 220 CE.

An Enduring Legacy

The Qin and Han dynasties brought tremendous political, cultural, economic, and social changes. The central government grew in power and authority, and emperors were considered the link between heaven and earth. They were assisted by officials who were chosen for their abilities, rather than by aristocrats who inherited their positions.

A Han interpretation of Confucianism became the ideology that guided the empire. Emphasizing morality and humaneness, Confucianism inspired people to behave respectably and to view government service as an honorable calling. The Imperial Academy was open to boys of any social background, and by the middle of the second century was teaching classic Confucian texts to more than thirty thousand students a year.

Several Han emperors recognized agriculture as the "foundation of the empire" and issued edicts to promote it. Advances in tilling, planting, irrigation, and harvesting increased agricultural production so farmers could provide enough food for the whole population, freeing many men to serve as government officials and soldiers.

During the Han years other significant innovations sprang up in science, technology, transportation, textiles, medicine, mathematics, and weaponry. Many Chinese inventions—including paper, iron tools, the wheelbarrow, the parachute, and the rudder—did not appear in the West until centuries later. Major developments were also made in literature, music, and religion.

During the Qin and Han dynasties, separate states, ethnic groups, and cultures were melded into a unified empire. Tens of millions of people identified themselves as Chinese loyal to the emperor, sharing a culture based on Confucianism. This early model guided China all the way into the twentieth century.

Time Line of the Qin and Early Han Dynasties

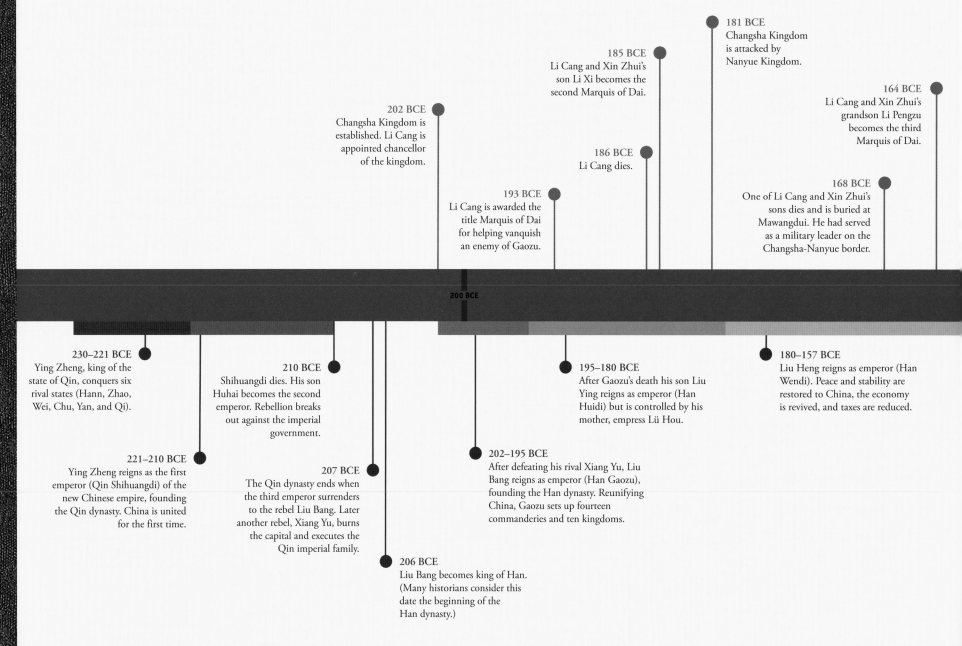

181 BCE
Changsha Kingdom is attacked by Nanyue Kingdom.

185 BCE
Li Cang and Xin Zhui's son Li Xi becomes the second Marquis of Dai.

164 BCE
Li Cang and Xin Zhui's grandson Li Pengzu becomes the third Marquis of Dai.

202 BCE
Changsha Kingdom is established. Li Cang is appointed chancellor of the kingdom.

186 BCE
Li Cang dies.

193 BCE
Li Cang is awarded the title Marquis of Dai for helping vanquish an enemy of Gaozu.

168 BCE
One of Li Cang and Xin Zhui's sons dies and is buried at Mawangdui. He had served as a military leader on the Changsha-Nanyue border.

200 BCE

230–221 BCE
Ying Zheng, king of the state of Qin, conquers six rival states (Hann, Zhao, Wei, Chu, Yan, and Qi).

210 BCE
Shihuangdi dies. His son Huhai becomes the second emperor. Rebellion breaks out against the imperial government.

195–180 BCE
After Gaozu's death his son Liu Ying reigns as emperor (Han Huidi) but is controlled by his mother, empress Lü Hou.

180–157 BCE
Liu Heng reigns as emperor (Han Wendi). Peace and stability are restored to China, the economy is revived, and taxes are reduced.

221–210 BCE
Ying Zheng reigns as the first emperor (Qin Shihuangdi) of the new Chinese empire, founding the Qin dynasty. China is united for the first time.

207 BCE
The Qin dynasty ends when the third emperor surrenders to the rebel Liu Bang. Later another rebel, Xiang Yu, burns the capital and executes the Qin imperial family.

202–195 BCE
After defeating his rival Xiang Yu, Liu Bang reigns as emperor (Han Gaozu), founding the Han dynasty. Reunifying China, Gaozu sets up fourteen commanderies and ten kingdoms.

206 BCE
Liu Bang becomes king of Han. (Many historians consider this date the beginning of the Han dynasty.)

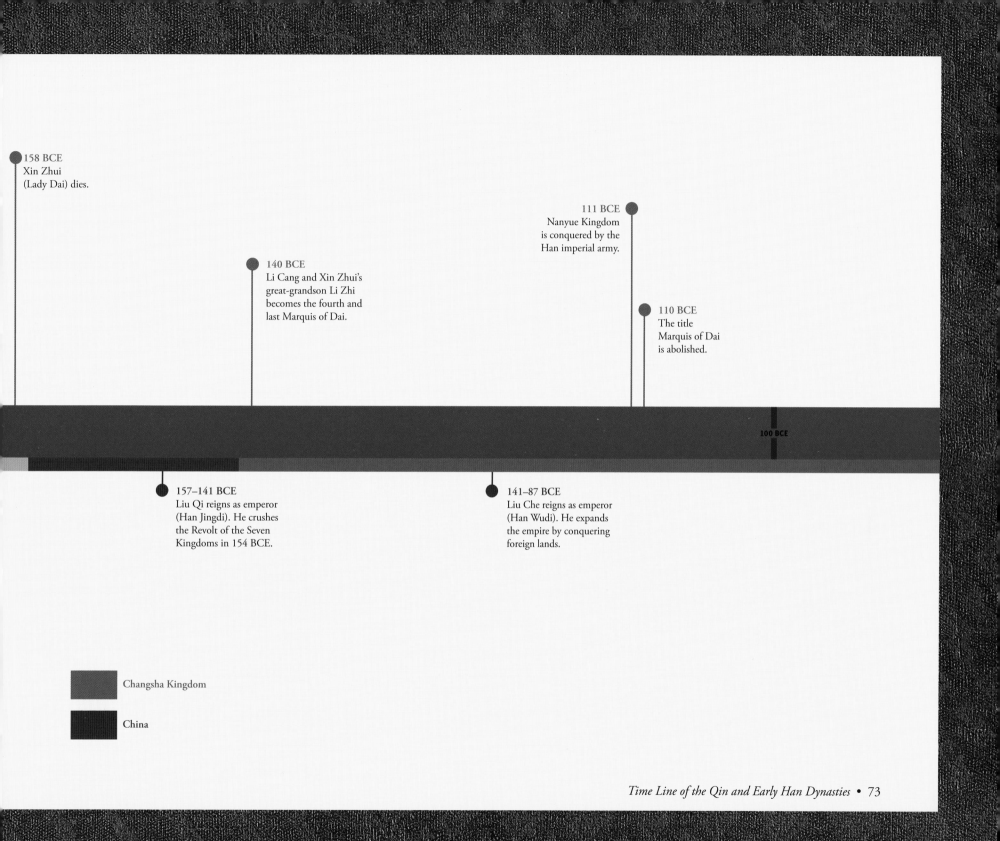

158 BCE
Xin Zhui
(Lady Dai) dies.

111 BCE
Nanyue Kingdom
is conquered by the
Han imperial army.

140 BCE
Li Cang and Xin Zhui's
great-grandson Li Zhi
becomes the fourth and
last Marquis of Dai.

110 BCE
The title
Marquis of Dai
is abolished.

100 BCE

157–141 BCE
Liu Qi reigns as emperor
(Han Jingdi). He crushes
the Revolt of the Seven
Kingdoms in 154 BCE.

141–87 BCE
Liu Che reigns as emperor
(Han Wudi). He expands
the empire by conquering
foreign lands.

Changsha Kingdom

China

Glossary

autopsy: Examination of a dead body to figure out what caused the death and, in the case of a pathological autopsy, what changes were caused by disease.

burial chamber: Large wooden vault divided into compartments and placed at the bottom of tomb pits in ancient China, such as those at Mawangdui. The middle compartment held the body, within a nested set of coffins, and the side compartments were for supplies, equipment, and personal possessions.

cadaver: Dead body, especially one used for study by doctors and scientists.

chancellor: Highest government official serving a king or emperor during early imperial China (also translated as "prime minister," "counselor-in-chief," or "premier").

Changsha (chahng-shah): A southern kingdom in the Han Empire, lasting from 202 BCE to 37 CE. Capital of modern Hunan Province.

coffin: Box for burying a dead body.

commandery: Province administered by a governor who was appointed by the central government.

Confucianism: Philosophy of Confucius, or Kong Qiu (kong chee-oh) (551–479 BCE), advocating the value of virtue in one's behavior, attitudes, and relationships with other people.

corpse: Dead body, especially of a human.

Daoism: As a philosophy, Daoism's fundamental principle is the Dao (Way) as the source of all that exists; Daoists seek to live in harmony with the Dao. As a religion, early Daoism focused on seeking immortality through the spiritual transcendence of physical limitations.

dynasty: Sequence of emperors who are members of the same family, such as the Liu family of the Han dynasty (206 BCE–220 CE).

emperor: Supreme ruler of an empire.

empire: A political unit composed of multiple states or territories ruled by a single monarch.

feiyi **(fay-yee):** A long silk painting laid on top of the innermost coffin in a tomb. Sometimes called a funeral banner or translated as "flying garment" or "flying banner."

geng **(guhng):** Souplike stew made of various combinations of vegetables, grain, meat, and fish. Most common main dish in ancient China.

Han (hahn) dynasty: Second dynasty of the Chinese empire. The Western Han dynasty lasted from 206 BCE to 6 CE. The Eastern Han dynasty lasted from 25 to 220 CE. These two periods are sometimes called the Former and the Later Han dynasties.

Han Gaozu (hahn gow*-dsoo): First emperor of the Han Empire (reigned 202 to 195 BCE); founder of the Han dynasty. Sometimes known as Han Gaodi (pronounced hahn gow-dee).

Huang-Lao (hwahng-low*): Branch of Daoism concerned with how a ruler governs successfully; popular with early Han emperors.

hun **(hwun):** Spiritual part of the soul, believed to leave the body after death.

Hunan (hoo-nahn): Province in south-central China. Changsha is its capital.

*Rhymes with *now.*

kingdom: State ruled by a monarch who can pass the rulership to an heir.

lacquer: A protective, decorative coating for wood, cloth, clay, or bamboo, made from the sap of lacquer trees.

Li Cang (lee tsahng): First chancellor of the Changsha Kingdom; first Marquis of Dai; buried at Mawangdui in 186 BCE. Sometimes known as Li Zhu Cang (lee joo tsahng).

Liu Bang (lyoo bahng): Personal name of Han Gaozu, first emperor of the Han dynasty. Also known as Liu Ji (lyoo jee).

liubo **(lyoo-bo-ah):** Popular board game in early China.

marquis (MAR-kwus or mar-KEE): An aristocratic rank in the early Han dynasty.

Mawangdui (mah-wahng-dway): Burial site in Changsha, Hunan Province, China, of three members of the Li family, including Li Cang (Marquis of Dai), Xin Zhui (Lady Dai), and their adult son. Excavated 1972–1974 CE.

mingqi **(ming-chee):** Nonfunctional clay or wooden models made to be buried in tombs. Includes models of servants, houses, animals, coins, and musical instruments.

Nanyue (nahn-yooeh): An independent kingdom from 203 to 111 BCE, when it was conquered by the Han Empire. Nanyue was located south of Changsha.

po **(po-ah):** Earthly part of the soul, believed to control the body and remain with it after death.

qi **(chee):** Life force or energy believed to permeate the natural world. Sometimes translated as "vapor," "breath," or "vital energy." Fundamental concept in traditional Chinese medicine.

qin **(chin):** String instrument plucked by the player's fingers. The *qin* in the son's tomb at Mawangdui was 32.4 inches (82.4 centimeters) long with seven silk strings attached to tuning pegs.

Qin (chin) dynasty: First dynasty of the Chinese Empire, lasting from 221 to 207 BCE.

Qin Shihuangdi (chin sher-hwahng-dee): First emperor of a unified China (reigned 221 to 210 BCE); founder of the Qin dynasty. His personal name was Ying Zheng (ying jeng) or Zhao Zheng (jao jeng).

se **(suh):** Large wooden string instrument plucked with the fingers.

state: A political community under a central government.

territory: A region under the authority of an external government.

tomb: A place for burying a dead body, particularly a large structure dug underground or cut into rock.

Xin Zhui (shin jway): Personal name of Lady Dai, wife of Li Cang. Scholars believe she died at age 54 and was buried at Mawangdui in 158 BCE.

yu **(yee-oo):** Large mouth organ; a reed wind instrument.

Author's Note

I first learned of the Mawangdui tombs in November 1999, at a special exhibit at the National Palace Museum in Taipei, Taiwan. Seeing objects of the Li family's daily life and then staring at a model of Lady Dai "sleeping" created for me an irresistible connection to her. I was gripped by the vivid awareness that Lady Dai had been an actual person who had combed her hair, suffered illnesses, and enjoyed good food and music.

My desire to learn more about the Li family and their world led me to track down materials of all kinds on Mawangdui and on life in the early Han dynasty. I prowled university libraries for articles, haunted bookstores in American and Asian cities, scoured websites, and was spellbound by videos. Every source's bibliography launched a search to track down its sources.

In 2002 I traveled to the city of Changsha to see the tomb site, as well as Lady Dai and the artifacts in the Hunan Provincial Museum. Seeing the full range of artifacts impressed upon me so many new details—the astounding preservation of the two-thousand-year-old food, the glamour of the silk clothes, the massiveness of the burial chamber timbers. Seeing Lady Dai's actual body was mesmerizing.

The next year I published an article, "Silk Treasures of Mawangdui," in *Dig* magazine. But writing one article wasn't enough to satisfy my curiosity; I wanted to keep exploring by writing a book about the tombs.

Pieces of information about Mawangdui lay scattered about my mind like pieces of a jigsaw puzzle. How could I fit them together into a book? Finally I recognized that the Mawangdui tombs are like a time capsule: every artifact reveals something about life in the early Han dynasty. Each artifact tells a story—what it meant to the mourners who buried it, how it expresses the artisans' knowledge and skills, and what it was like to live in that time and place. Within this framework I could not only describe the Mawangdui artifacts but also explore the history and culture of the early Han dynasty.

This expedition has lasted fourteen years so far, yet my fascination with Mawangdui and Lady Dai is as intense as ever. Next? I would love to go back to Changsha to see the artifacts and tomb site again, and to silently thank Lady Dai and her family for inspiring my marvelous journey through time.

A Note About Imagined Scenes

Chapters 2 through 6 each open with an illustration and an imagined scene that are based on fact—on artifacts found in the tombs or on historical research. These are meant to give readers a sense of "being there" with Lady Dai during her lifetime.

Acknowledgments

Unending thanks go to my father, Dr. Chien Liu, who traveled with me to Taipei and Changsha to see the artifacts and tomb site. He also tirelessly translated Chinese materials for me.

I am indebted to Dr. Peng Long-xiang (leader of the autopsy team), the late Mr. Hou Liang (head of the excavation team), the Hunan Provincial Museum (especially Mr. Huang Lei, Ms. Hou Yan, Ms. Chen Mi, and Ms. Sun Lingling), and expert reviewers Ms. Yu Yanjiao of the Hunan Provincial Museum and Dr. Margarete Prüch of the Institute of East Asian Art History at the University of Heidelberg, Germany. Any errors that remain, however, are mine.

I am grateful to the team at Charlesbridge—including my phenomenal editor, Alyssa Mito Pusey; designer Martha MacLeod Sikkema; and artist Sarah S. Brannen—for supporting my dream for this book.

Heartfelt thanks go to Mike, Steffi, and Mindy, who helped in ways both practical and intangible, and who lived with my ups and downs as I worked on this book.

Sources of Quotations

For further information on sources, see the selected bibliography on pages 78–79.

Chapter 1
Page 9: "I joked . . . actually happen." Hou Liang in Hou Liang, *Chenfengde wenming,* p. 8 (translation by Chien Liu).

Page 9: "These young . . . bamboo baskets." Hou Liang in ibid., p. 8 (translation by Chien Liu).

Page 11: "Look at that!" Wang Yuyu as retold by Hou Liang, quoted in Zhang Dongxia, ed., "The Legend of Mawangdui," p. 56.

Page 12: "as soft . . . rotted away." Hou Liang, quoted in ibid., p. 58.

Chapter 2
Page 21: "only . . . an adult." From Peng Long-xiang in email to author, October 27, 2006.

Page 21: "I wasn't . . . woman died." Peng Long-xiang in ibid.

Page 21: "differs from . . . in the past." In Hunan Medical College, ed., "Study of an Ancient Cadaver in Mawangtui Tomb No. 1 of the Han Dynasty in Changsha (Summary)," p. 342.

Page 25: "best . . . in the world." From various sources, including "Chinese Lady Dai: Best Preserved Body in the World," *China View,* August 25, 2004, http://news.xinhuanet.com/english/ 2004-08/25/content_1879594.htm.

Page 25: "Mawangdui-type cadaver." From various sources, including Peng Long-xiang and Wu Zhong-bi, "The Mawangtui-Type Cadavers in China," p. 329.

Chapter 3
Page 29: "Filial piety . . . civilization." Confucius, as quoted in "The Classic of Filial Piety," trans. Patricia Buckley Ebrey, in Ebrey, ed., *Chinese Civilization: A Sourcebook,* 2nd ed., (New York: Free Press, 1993), p. 64.

Chapter 4
Page 35: "For the beauty . . . rocks!" From "'The Lord of the East' (Dong jun)," in Qu Yuan et al., *The Songs of the South: An Ancient Chinese Anthology of Poems by Qu Yuan and Other Poets,* trans. David Hawkes (Harmondsworth, UK: Penguin, 1985), p. 113.

Page 43: "All your household . . . roll." From "Zhao hun 'Summons of the Soul'" in ibid., pp. 227–28.

Chapter 6
Page 59: "Monkey Bawling . . . Hotness." In Donald J. Harper, *Early Chinese Medical Literature,* p. 315.

Historical Note
Page 65: "He killed . . . all." Fan Kuai, quoted in Sima Qian, *Records of the Grand Historian: Han Dynasty I,* p. 31.

Pages 66–67: "The emperor . . . lies." The scholars Hou and Lu, quoted in Szuma Chien, *Selections from Records of the Historian,* trans. Yang Hsien-yi and Gladys Yang (Beijing: Foreign Languages Press, 1979), pp. 180–81.

Page 67: "For a long . . . over you." Han Gaozu, quoted in Sima Qian, *Records of the Grand Historian: Han Dynasty I,* p. 62.

Page 67: "Your Majesty . . . horseback?" Lu Jia, quoted in ibid., p. 226.

Page 69: "if the laws . . . obedient." Han Wendi, quoted in ibid., p. 291.

Page 69: "I have . . . single day." Han Wendi, quoted in ibid., p. 304.

Page 71: "foundation of the empire." In Cho-yun Hsu, *Han Agriculture: The Formation of Early Chinese Agrarian Economy (206 B.C.–220 A.D.),* (Seattle: University of Washington Press, 1980), pp. 167, 169, 170.

Selected Bibliography

I consulted more than four hundred sources—especially official reports, eyewitness accounts, research findings from experts, and translations of classic Chinese texts. The following sources were most helpful to me:

Website: Hunan Provincial Museum
http://www.hnmuseum.com/hnmuseum/eng/
- To find photos and descriptions of the Li family, their tombs, and artifacts, click on "Exhibition & Activity" then "Permanent Exhibition" then "Cultural Relics from Mawangdui Han Tombs."
- For photos and descriptions of individual artifacts, click on "Collection" then "Database" then "Cultural Relics from the Mawangdui Tombs."

Books and Articles

Bahn, Paul, ed. *Written in Bones: How Human Remains Unlock the Secrets of the Dead.* Buffalo, NY: Firefly Books, 2003.

Buck, David D. "Three Han Dynasty Tombs at Ma-wang-tui." *World Archaeology* 7, no. 1 (1975): 30–45.

Chang, Chun-shu. *The Rise of the Chinese Empire.* Vol. 1, *Nation, State, and Imperialism in Early China, ca. 1600 B.C.–A.D. 8.* Ann Arbor, MI: University of Michigan Press, 2007.

Chen Jianming, ed. *Noble Tombs at Mawangdui: Art and Life of the Changsha Kingdom, Third Century B.C.E. to First Century C.E.* Changsha, China: Yuelu Publishing House, 2008.

Chow, Fong, and Cheng Yeh. "A Brief Report on the Excavation of Han Tomb No. 1 at Ma-wang-tui, Ch'ang-sha." *Artibus Asiae* 35, no. 1/2 (1973): 15–24.

Fu Juyou and Chen Songchang. "A Comprehensive Introduction About the Cultural Relics Unearthed from the Han Tombs at Mawangdui." In *Mawangdui Han mu wenwu* [The Cultural Relics Unearthed from the Han Tombs at Mawangdui], volume supplement. Changsha, China: Hunan Chubanshe [Hunan Publishing House], 1992.

Hardy, Grant, and Anne Behnke Kinney. *The Establishment of the Han Empire and Imperial China.* Westport, CT: Greenwood Press, 2005.

Harley, J. B., and David Woodward, eds. *The History of Cartography.* Vol. 2, bk. 2, *Cartography in the Traditional East and Southeast Asian Societies.* Chicago: University of Chicago Press, 1994.

Harper, Donald J. *Early Chinese Medical Literature: The Mawangdui Medical Manuscripts.* London: Kegan Paul International, 1998.

Hou Liang. *Chenfengde wenming: Shenmide Mawangdui Han mu* [Mysterious Mawangdui Han Tomb: The Culture Under the Dust and Earth]. Changsha, China: Hunan Renmin Chubanshe, 2002.

Hunan Medical College, ed. "Study of an Ancient Cadaver in Mawangtui Tomb No. 1 of the Han Dynasty in Changsha (Summary)." In *Changsha Mawangdui yihao Han mu gushi yanjiu* [Study of an Ancient Cadaver in Mawangtui Tomb No. 1 of the Han Dynasty in Changsha], 335–344. Beijing: Wenwu Chubanshe [Cultural Relics Publishing House], 1980.

Hunan Provincial Museum, and Institute of Archaeology, Academia Sinica. "The Han Tomb No. 1 at Mawangtui, Changsha (Abstract)." In *Changsha Mawangdui yihao Han mu* [The Han Tomb No. 1 at Mawangdui, Changsha], vol. 1, supplement, 1–9. Beijing: Wenwu Chubanshe [Cultural Relics Publishing House], 1973.

Hunan Sheng Bowuguan and Hunan Sheng Wenwu Kaogu Yanjiusuo [Hunan Provincial Museum, and Institute of Archaeology of Hunan Province]. *Changsha Mawangdui er, san hao Han mu* [Tombs 2 and 3 of the Han Dynasty at Mawangdui, Changsha]. Vol. 1, *Tianye kaogu fajue baogao* [Report on Excavation]. Beijing: Wenwu Chubanshe [Cultural Relics Publishing House], 2004.

Hunan Sheng Bowuguan and Zhongguo Kexueyuan Kaogu Yanjiusuo [Hunan Provincial Museum, and Institute of Archaeology, Chinese

Academy of Sciences]. *Changsha Mawangdui yihao Han mu* [The Han Tomb No. 1 at Mawangdui, Changsha]. 2 vols. Beijing: Wenwu Chubanshe [Cultural Relics Publishing House], 1973.

Institute of the History of Natural Sciences, and Chinese Academy of Sciences. *Ancient China's Technology and Science.* Beijing: Foreign Languages Press, 1983.

Loewe, Michael. *Chinese Ideas of Life and Death: Faith, Myth and Reason in the Han Period (202 BC–AD 220).* Taipei, Taiwan: SMC Publishing, 1994. First published 1982 by Allen & Unwin.

——. *Ways to Paradise: The Chinese Quest for Immortality.* Taipei, Taiwan: SMC Publishing, 1994. First published 1979 by Allen & Unwin.

Nylan, Michael, and Michael Loewe, eds. *China's Early Empires: A Re-appraisal.* Cambridge: Cambridge University Press, 2010.

Peng Long-xiang. "Study of an Ancient Cadaver Excavated from a Han Dynasty (207 B.C.–A.D. 220) Tomb in Hunan Province." Paper presented at the Proceedings of the I World Congress on Mummy Studies, Tenerife, Canary Islands, Spain, February 3–6, 1992.

Peng Long-xiang and Wu Zhong-bi. "The Mawangtui-Type Cadavers in China." In *Mummies, Disease & Ancient Cultures,* 2nd ed., edited by Aidan Cockburn, Eve Cockburn, and Theodore A. Reyman, 328–335. Cambridge: Cambridge University Press, 1998.

Pirazzoli-t'Serstevens, Michèle. *The Han Dynasty.* Translated by Janet Seligman. New York: Rizzoli, 1982.

Sima Qian. *Records of the Grand Historian: Han Dynasty I.* Translated by Burton Watson. Rev. ed., vol. 1. Hong Kong: Research Centre for Translation, Chinese University of Hong Kong; Columbia University Press, 1993.

——. *Records of the Grand Historian: Qin Dynasty.* Translated by Burton Watson. Rev. ed. Hong Kong: Research Centre for Translation, Chinese University of Hong Kong; New York: Columbia University Press, 1993.

Steele, John, ed. *The I-Li or Book of Etiquette and Ceremonial.* Vol. 2. London: Probsthain & Co., 1917.

Tsien, Tsuen-hsuin. *Written on Bamboo & Silk: The Beginnings of Chinese Books & Inscriptions.* 2nd ed. Chicago: University of Chicago Press, 2004.

Twitchett, Denis, and Michael Loewe, eds. *The Cambridge History of China.* Vol. 1, *The Ch'in and Han Empires, 221 B.C.–A.D. 220.* Taipei, Taiwan: Caves Books, 1987. First published 1986 by Cambridge University Press.

Waley-Cohen, Joanna, trans. *The Lacquers of the Mawangdui Tomb.* Hong Kong: Millennia Limited, 1984.

Wang Zhongshu. *Han Civilization.* Translated by K. C. Chang and others. New Haven, CT: Yale University Press, 1982.

Wieczorek, Alfried, and Wilfried Rosendahl, eds. *Mummies of the World.* Munich: Prestel, 2010.

Wu Hung. *The Art of the Yellow Springs: Understanding Chinese Tombs.* Honolulu, HI: University of Hawai'i Press, 2010.

Yü, Ying-shih. "Han China." In *Food in Chinese Culture: Anthropological and Historical Perspectives,* edited by K. C. Chang, 53–83. Taipei, Taiwan: SMC Publishing, 1997. First published 1977 by Yale University Press.

Zhang Dongxia, ed. "The Legend of Mawangdui." In *The Legend of Mawangdui: A Recount of the Past and a Revealing of the Secrets,* 50–83. Beijing: China Intercontinental Press, 2007.

NOTE: A full bibliography, divided by topics, is available at **www.ChristineLiuPerkins.com/Mawangdui.**

Index

afterlife beliefs, 28–29, 49–50; *see also* souls
autopsy, 20–23

bamboo strips, 37, 54, 55, 61
bodies, 20–25, 29–30
books
  destruction of, 55–56, 61
  early Chinese, 55–56
  Han libraries, 61
  in son's tomb, 54; *see also* "hidden library"
burial chamber; *see also* tombs
  compartments, 10, 11, 13, 30–32, 36–37, 39, 54
  as house for soul, 28, 29, 30–32, 36, 43

calling-back ceremony, 26, 27, 30, 43, 49
chancellor, 15, 16, 68, 72
Changsha, 15, 16, 60, 68, 72–73
coffin of Lady Dai
  body in, 12, 13, 24–25, 30, 47
  fluid in, 12, 24–25, 51
  nested layers of, 11–12, 13, 30
  paintings on, 11–12, 13, 28, 29, 30
  silk *feiyi* in, 13, 28, 48–50
comets, 56, 57
Confucianism, 41, 70–71
Confucius, 29

Daoism, 57–58

divination, 30, 43, 54, 55, 56–57

emperors, 65–71, 72–73
excavation, 8–11, 14–15
exercise, 59
expansion of China, 64, 69–70, 73

feiyi, 13, 28, 48–51
filial piety, 29–30, 33
food
  afterlife beliefs and, 29, 33, 43
  and agricultural economy, 69, 70, 71
  Han cuisine, 34, 35, 37
  in imagined scenes, 18, 19, 34, 35
  in Lady Dai's tomb, 5, 32, 36–37
  muskmelon, 18, 19, 22
funeral rituals, 29–33, 49–50

games, 5, 42–43, 62
geng (stew), 35, 37
grave preparation, 29, 30–33
Great Wall of China, 64, 66

Han dynasty
  Daoism, 57–58
  emperors of, 67–71, 72–73
  establishment of, 67–68, 72
  expansion of China, 64, 69–70, 73
  food in; *see* food
  imperial library, 61
  legacy of, 17, 70–71
  maps of China, 16, 64
  music in; *see* musicians and instruments
  "time capsule," 17, 33,

62–63, 76
  time line, 72–73
  Western and Eastern, 70
Han Gaozu, 67–68, 72
Han Huidi, 15, 16, 68, 72
Han Jingdi, 69, 70, 73
Han Wendi, 57–58, 68–69, 72–73
Han Wudi, 67, 69–70, 73
"hidden library"
  Daoism texts, 57–58
  divination books, 56–57
  historical value of, 54, 56, 58, 61
  lacquer box in tomb, 54
  maps, 14, 54, 60
  medical books, 58–59
Hou Liang, 9, 76
Huang-Lao, 57–58
Hunan Provincial Museum, 4–5, 8, 11, 76

imagined scenes
  banquet, 34, 35
  calling-back ceremony, 26, 27
  explanation of, 76
  Lady Dai's death, 18, 19
  silk production, 44, 45
  son's military career, 52, 53
Imperial Academy, 69–71

jia (home or family), 11

lacquerware
  box in son's tomb, 54
  in imagined scenes, 18, 34, 35
  lacquer production, 38
  in Lady Dai's tomb, 5, 11, 32, 36, 38–39
  photographs of, 36, 38

Lady Dai, Xin Zhui
  autopsy, 20–23
  body of, 4, 12, 13, 17, 20–25, 30, 47
  death of, 17, 18, 19, 22, 27
  feast in tomb of, 32, 36–37, 43
  grave preparation and funeral, 29, 30–32
  health of, 17, 19, 21–22
  identity of, 12, 15, 17
  museum exhibit, 4–5, 23, 24, 76
  noble lifestyle of, 36, 38, 46–47, 62, 69; *see also* imagined scenes
  preparation for afterlife, 24, 25, 30
  time line, 72–73
Li, Son [of Li Cang and Xin Zhui]
  artifacts in tomb of, 5, 14, 28, 40, 42, 51, 54; *see also* "hidden library"
  food in tomb of, 37
  identity of, 14, 17, 60
  liubo, in tomb of, 5, 42–43, 62
  military career, 14, 52, 53, 60, 61, 72
  tomb of, 14, 69
Li Cang, 15–17, 62, 66, 68, 69, 72, 73
Liu family; *see specific Han emperors*
liubo, 5, 42–43, 62

maps
  found in tomb, 14, 54, 60
  Han dynasty, 16, 64
  multiple uses for, 61
  Qin dynasty, 64
Marquis of Dai, 12, 15–17, 68, 72–73

Mawangdui hills, 7–8
Mawangdui-type cadavers, 21, 25
mingqi (spirit objects), 29, 31–32, 36, 39–41
musicians and instruments
  funeral and grave preparation, 31–32
  in Han culture, 34, 35, 38, 40–41, 43
  in the tombs, 40, 41, 48
  zithers, 5, 34, 35, 40, 41, 43
muskmelon, 18, 19, 22

naming conventions, 12, 67

Peng, Long-xiang, 20–21, 76

qi, 29, 58, 59
Qin dynasty, 64, 65–67, 70–71, 72
Qin Shihuangdi, 65–67, 68, 72

Roman Empire, 17, 46, 61, 69

signature seals, 12, 15, 32, 62
silk
  body wrappings, 12, 13, 47, 51
  books and documents, 54–56, 58, 60
  clothing illustrations, 18, 26, 34, 44, 52
  clothing in Han culture, 4, 35, 38, 39, 46–47
  coffin adornment, 12, 13, 47
  feiyi, 13, 28, 48–51

in Lady Dai's burial chamber, 32, 36, 38, 40, 48, 50, 51
  production, 44, 45, 46–47, 51
  shields, 46
  value of, 46, 55
silkworms, 44, 45, 46–47
souls
  banquet for, 32, 36–37, 43
  entertainment for, 32, 40–43
  hun and *po,* 28–29, 30
  journey of, 28–30, 50
  servants for, 32, 36, 39
  "summoning of," 26, 27, 30, 43, 49
  tomb supplies for, 29, 31–32, 43
"Summons of the Soul" (poem), 43

"time capsule," 17, 33, 62–63, 76
tombs
  clay/charcoal layers, 9–11, 24, 25, 32–33
  damage to, 14, 17
  discovery of, 7–8, 14
  excavation of, 8–11, 14–15
  grave preparation, 30–32
  layout of, 6
  on map of China, 16

wart remedies, 59
writing surfaces, 37, 54–55, 61

Xin Zhui; *see* Lady Dai, Xin Zhui

zithers, 5, 34, 35, 40, 41, 43